MW00776151

RAMBLINGS
ON ROCK SPRINGS ROAD

by Gilbert Gordon

Cover Design and Illustrated by Carter Gordon
Published by BookBaby

Published by BookBaby

Print ISBN: 978-1-09837-172-2

Printed in the United States of America

I love it! It's so Gilbert: humor, moments of poignancy, his observations, use of imagery, metaphor. It's truly wonderful! Thank you for giving me the gift of your writing. —Jeff Lynk

Your book made me laugh out loud, and then I found myself crying. I think this is the first time a book provided this gift for me. You struck many nerves. I need ten more copies. —Bud George

What courage it must have taken to bring into the open such intimate vulnerabilities. Upon arrival, Ramblings stole time from me that I would have thought not available. —Thom Puckett

Your words have a way of enveloping my attention and imagination, and I am transported. I simply enjoy reading it, and I find it hard to put down- and that, in my opinion, is the highest praise a book can receive. —Alyssa Manweiler

I just finished Ramblings. It is a beautiful book, and you are a gifted writer. I need four additional copies for my friends. — Steve Bartholomew

Ramblings is classic Gilbert Gordon: raw, gritty, soulful. —Pam Singer

I just finished your book, and I loved it. I particularly appreciated your writing style-the way you pepper your work with humor, education, and humility. You definitely need to write another one. —Marie Claire Turrentine

Since my writing will fail to express why the tears are in my eyes right now, let me just say that your book is golden. I loved it. There is much to be remembered, desperately to be remembered. Thank you for reminding me not to miss or brush aside the profound things in the simplicity of day to day life. —Polly Ricks

This book has made its way into our hearts. Some sections were reread where we were moved by your giftedness. —Carney Farris

I just finished your book, and I cannot begin to convey what I'm feeling inside. Your writing is incredibly personal and honest, and each chapter was like looking into your soul. You have given me a treasure. —Jane Carrigan

I just finished Gilbert's book! I've been savoring a chapter, here and there- not wanting to finish it. Oh, wow! It's not just the stories but the writing style. I will be reading it again. —Elizabeth Shrum

Few writers reveal their thought processes, warts, and all, like you did in this book, and it was a delight. —Alan Miller

Your storytelling ability has left me devouring your book in one day. —Abby Douglass

I never cry, but I cried throughout the book and laughed out loud. I want ten more copies for my reading group. —Rachel Wheat

AUTHOR'S NOTE

As caretaker of our family cemetery, I read the names of my ancestors as I cut around the headstones. There are farmers, doctors, writers, athletes, state representatives, poets, lawyers, soldiers from four wars, rebels, and children. They range in age from a few days to a century. Their epitaphs reveal only the vitals, the alpha and the omega, and I want to know more. I stand in front of each grave, asking many questions and wondering how similar their lives were to my own. When I join them, I want to leave behind something of myself so others who keep the cemetery will not wonder so much about my life, as inconsequential as it may be.

Soon after my mother died in 2014, I wrote a chapter each month for a year as a reminder for my siblings of the wonderful life we experienced together in spite of the many difficulties we encountered. I had written these, in part, over a forty-year span, not finishing any of them until then. Included were stories of our ancestors, which I shared not only with my sisters and brother but also with our children. Then Ginny, my wife, encouraged me to put the chapters in a sequence that might be enjoyable for those outside of the family.

I rushed to print part one of this book a year ago because my father-in-law was dying of bladder cancer. He is one of my heroes, and I wanted him to read it because he loved literature and read incessantly. He started it, but his health declined rapidly to the point that his wife came to the rescue and read the remainder, one chapter each night. To hear my words read and enjoyed by this special couple is a treasure I will never forget. Days before his death, as I was sitting at the foot of his bed, he remarked to me that he loved Ramblings because it was an honest book. Since he was a man of integrity and never stooped to flattery, his comment is one of the most endearing compliments I received about the book. Now I have completed part two. After revising part one, both are published together because it feels more complete; one needs the other.

I am not a Southern writer. That genre, as I was taught in high school, belongs to the likes of William Faulkner and his stories about a fading Southern aristocracy, or to Harper Lee and her "tired, old town" which found itself in the age-old dilemma of social injustice. This is not a story about the South. There is no aristocracy, no tired town, no moral dilemma. It is a story about a road in the South and the relationships found there in family, neighbors, and community, and how they impacted my life. These people were and are important to me. They were not perfect, but importance is better than perfection. The frailties of these people make them wholly human and partly saint. This book is the only remaining means I have to honor them.

I have made no effort to validate certain aspects of some of the stories that were told to me or as I remember them. They are, with a touch of embellishment, as I envision them through the rose-colored glasses I wear. If, by adding some measure of twisted truth, I have given the reader a more accurate view of the character, then so be it.

Sitting on our front porch in the evening, Ginny and I listen to the creek as it rolls along. We hear the bullfrogs and the synchronized chirps of crickets in the pond. Occasionally a hoot-owl sounds off in the distance, and as the sun sets, the coyotes start their nightly vigil. It is a symphony. But not everyone appreciates these sounds. Others may prefer a different beat. So it is with literature. My hope is that as this book is read, some will join us in the evening on our front porch to enjoy the sound of the words in bringing to life the colorful personalities I have been privileged to know on Rock Springs Road.

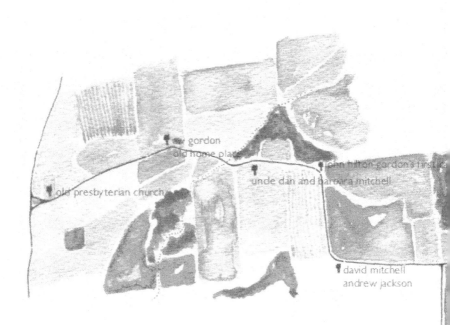

mallard house

charles and catherine gordon
gilbert's birthplace

miss eunice

PART ONE

PROLOGUE

The 1972 Summer Olympics had ended. I watched the closing festivities on our TV late that evening. Everyone else had retired for the night and were fast asleep; milking the cows still came at four o'clock in the morning. When the glow of the TV finally faded away I sat alone in the quiet, but I still heard the deafening roar of the crowd. In total darkness, I felt confetti showering down upon me like snow. Sitting on the couch that night, I walked proudly to the winner's podium and put my hand over my heart as the National Anthem played. I was fourteen years old. The world had not yet shackled me with boundaries, so dreams were only postponed realities. My dream that night was to win a gold medal at the 1976 Olympic Summer Games in the 880-yard run, just as Dave Wottle had miraculously done. All I needed was a pair of work boots, a track, and four years of dedication. I would prepare for this amazing feat on Rock Springs Road where I lived.

The next morning, after milking the cows, I proceeded to the road to measure the 880 yards. My stride registered about three feet if I stretched a bit, so I stepped it off from directly in front of my house down to where an electric line ran across the road to another pole. The line was, appropriately for my dreams, covered with laurel. I decided to ride a bike on my first attempt to feel the wind in my face and gauge the necessary speed. I put air in the tires on my old one-speed bike. I swung my leg over and positioned my rump on the rusty seat. Described as butt-less, I was virtually bone on metal. Unlike the modern cyclist who dresses in fashionable spandex garb, riding with head down, gobbling up miles of asphalt in an attempt to maintain the perfect physique on a carbon-fibered biped, my bike was what was called a lift-your-eyes-toward-heaven type, with handle bars that made me sit up straight so I could actually see and enjoy the countryside. It was my sister's hand-me-down, so it did not have the high center bar indicative of true manliness.

Questions welled up in my mind. *What would I wear in competition?* Dave Wottle wore a controversial golfing cap. It was his trademark. Maybe I would wear a pair of overalls. That would surely set me apart. After all, the overall was formal attire on the farm. I bent down and felt the tires. They were tight, and I was ready for my maiden run down Rock Springs Road. I gripped the handles as my eyes narrowed and grew fierce. It was time. I started the stopwatch. My legs exploded like thunder, and my body struck like lightning. I felt the strain on the chain, as it seemed sure to snap under the exertion of my feet. Accelerating until I reached maximum velocity, I held it firm, barreling down the road in search of the gold medal.

Reflecting on the glory and honor of a world-class runner, I heard the unmistakable introduction to ABC TV's *Wide World of Sports. Could I remain humble in my success, or would record-breaking get the best of me?* My decision to be myself when showered with praise and admiration triumphed. *Difficult surely, but four years should be ample time to work on the humility part. Yes, I would accept the medal with grace and humility.*

The beautiful countryside was a blur as I zipped along, but I recognized every detail without looking, because in fourteen years some things become a part of you. I knew when I passed the house where a serial killer terrorized a farming community in the 1920s. Then, just around the corner, I felt the noose around the neck of my great-great grandfather during the Civil War as he barely avoided being hanged by way of a peach pie. I passed my grandfather's home, and the creek where we fished. I pedaled by the pet cemetery where my sisters and I presided over multiple funerals. I sped past the log house where Andrew Jackson spent time before making his way to the War of 1812. Finally, I passed the graveyard where six generations of Gordons were buried. So much history, and I was fortunate enough to have been born here.

I leaned against the curve and found myself only yards from the finish line. Pedaling furiously, I surged under the electronic photo-finish wire of laurel. It would be important to remember my family if I was interviewed after the race. I couldn't take all the credit. That is what any respectable All-American athlete would do. Perhaps even a comment on farm life. People like to hear about simple people doing extraordinary feats. I pictured my face on a box of Wheaties.

Coasting further down the road, I checked my stopwatch to validate my record-breaking pace. Staring in disbelief and confusion, my reasoning abilities struggled to acknowledge the obvious: Tempus fugit, but I had not. My watch was only a Timex, but it had never deceived me before. *How could it be that my speed on a bike was slower than Dave Wottle's speed on foot?* God grant me the serenity to accept the things I cannot change. I am a dreamer, but even I know the difference between a dream and a wish. I quickly looked around to see if anyone was watching … or laughing. The bike coasted slower and slower, as did my ego.

No medals, no interviews, no endorsements, no false humility. Nothing remained but an exhausted body and a crushed dream. As I finally rolled to a halt, the silence was too much. The stadium that had been filled with thousands of enthusiastic spectators, waving their arms in jubilant frenzy, was now a field of corn stalks, their dry leaves blowing in the hot wind. The barriers that lined both sides of the track to keep the crowd restrained were once again rusty, web-wired fences. The laurel I had just passed beneath was actually poison ivy, and the confetti that should have showered upon me was only the dry, swirling dust of a drought-ridden August day. The Olympic track was again only Rock Springs Road.

It was a long way home on the bike that day, retracing my failed journey. It was difficult just keeping my head lifted and, while gazing downward, I noticed my old, blown-out pair of work boots with my big toe frantically trying to exit. I saw my blue jeans that were six inches too short. My holey white tube socks sagged from lack of elastic. I felt older than I wanted to be, and reality was taking full shape.

I parked the bike on our breezeway and slowly plodded to the fence overlooking a field behind our house. Grazing cows kept the grass short that time of year, and my glazed eyes stared unconsciously into the distance. I was searching inside myself for greener pastures, as we are apt to do under such circumstances. Then I noticed small, green patches scattered here and there in the pasture where cows had defecated the previous year. Given a season, the manure had decomposed, providing nutrition and yielding the greener bits of pasture.

We spend much of our lives desperately looking over fences for something better. We grow anxious and desire a different life, when all along what we are trying to escape is exactly the catalyst that pushes us to reach our deepest longings. If we stay put, the difficulties nourish us and we become the greener pasture. Shit and failure have this in common: Given time, they yield something better. The humiliating defeat of a bike ride forced me to see what I already possessed, that the rich life I was privy to on Rock Springs Road made any medal inconsequential. The cedar glades, the deep pools along the creek, the colorful characters, the animals, the neighbors, family, traditions, and the bizarre stories of the generations all contributed to a host of medals.

This is the story of my people and their influence on me. I no longer bike down Rock Springs Road, but I still drive it. Most of the people are gone now. My boyhood farm was sold. Houses fill the horizon where we grew corn and alfalfa. The barns are in disrepair, the ponds are mostly filled in, and the old lanes are hardly recognizable. But on any given night, I can close my eyes and see it all, smell it all, and hear everything. These are the stories of those few short, wonder-years we call youth. This is how I heard and perceived them, how I lived and processed them, and eventually how I stored them away in my memory as a keepsake.

CHAPTER ONE

Forty-five miles southeast of Nashville, a road winds for four miles in the Central Basin of Rutherford County, Tennessee, connecting two larger, parallel roads. One road, the Shelbyville Pike, connects Murfreesboro to Shelbyville and was the route taken by the retreating Confederate Army after the defeat at Stones River. The other, Midland Road, was the most popular route from Nashville to New Orleans, the one traveled by Andrew Jackson en route to the Battle of New Orleans in the War of 1812. Stuck lazily between these two historic roads meanders the Rock Springs Road, where my ancestors settled and where I live today.

As the name of the road implies, there are rocks. Not those pretty, little shiny pebbles found scattered about on seashores and easily placed in a pocket. These massive limestone outcroppings rise above the surface a couple of feet, resembling the teeth of some Frost Monster of Norse mythology anchored somewhere in Middle Earth. Sometimes the outcroppings lie only inches beneath the surface, covered by a thin layer of silt, fooling my ancestors into believing they had selected a fertile home for their families. Around the periphery of every field lie piles of huge limestone fragments broken off by generations of plowing. When Joshua crossed the River Jordan, he piled up rocks so the Israelites would not forget the faithfulness of God in the Promised Land. When the Gordons crossed Dry Fork Creek to settle, they piled up rocks cursing and swearing under their breaths as plow shank after plow shank snapped. Zion existed only as a distant dream.

Where the rocks represented everything gone wrong in a fallen world, the springs provided proof that God still cared. Those deep pools never ran dry, and when the heat of late summer sapped the very moisture from our bones we made our way to the deep blue holes where the springs originated. The mystery of those bottom-less, watery pits intrigued me greatly. I imagined this was the place where Jules Verne's Otto Lidenbrock would someday surface from twenty-thousand leagues beneath. These eternal springs gave us hope that whatever happened in the world, we would always have water here on the farm. We kept an old metal cup tied with baling twine on a tree. Often, while cutting hay in the north forty, I parked the tractor in the shade alongside the bank of the creek, took that cup down, and dipped it into one of those icy cold springs. Cold water on a hot day has a powerful flavor of its own.

The rocks and the springs accompany the road, winding through cedar glades and passing over two creeks, bending through four ninety-degree turns before exiting in the familiar outcropping at the other end. Curves in a road indicate an attempt to find enough good soil to build upon, and Rock Springs Road resembles a snake. Traces of ancestors are evident by the cemeteries that pepper the roadside, where families took care of their own from cradle to grave.

Genealogies resemble the videos of a recent family vacation: no one is interested. But some background helps to provide a foundation to the larger story. In the South, our ancestors are always watching, and we include them in our conversations so as not to hurt their feelings. This is especially true if one lives in the Family Home and keeps the Family Cemetery. I have a responsibility and duty to briefly mention them in order to validate their existence, keeping them in the family consciousness and out of my bedroom at night.

So we came from Scotland via the Atlantic to the Carolina coast around 1750 after a shipwreck orphaned a young, lone survivor named Tommy Tatum. He later became the great-grandfather of John Hilton Gordon, the proclaimed patriarch of the Gordon family. Why Tommy left Scotland can only be surmised, but when he arrived and swam to shore, there were no border-control officers waiting and no walls prohibiting his entry. No proof of birth was necessary, as a man's presence was generally acceptable. He was an immigrant, and received no fanfare upon arrival. They never do. He stepped upon a new continent, and although he was one hundred percent Scottish, he became one hundred percent American, an invasive species as the Native Americans may have viewed him.

Tommy married Polly and begat William, who begat Elizabeth, who begat Margaret, who married John Hilton Gordon in 1832. Margaret had a premonition once when she turned over a rock on the first day of May and uncovered a frog lying beside nine crickets. She later married the old toad and birthed nine children. Virtually nothing is known of this couple's life together. Unlike today, where recording and documenting every moment of our mundane lives holds sway over living it, nine children and a Civil War kept them preoccupied.

John Hilton Gordon, my great-great-great grandfather (the toad previously mentioned) moved from North Carolina. Thirty years before Abraham Lincoln signed the Emancipation Proclamation freeing the slaves in the South during the Civil War, John Hilton freed his nine slaves—a very unpopular decision in the South at the time—and was forced to leave his home there. He ended up on Rock Springs Road, married Margaret, and raised eight sons and a daughter in a one-room log house only a short distance from Dry Fork Creek where I now live.

When the Civil War followed him to Middle Tennessee, it also came to his back door when a group of Union soldiers arrived, dragged him to a nearby tree, and prepared to hang him. They were hungry, but he refused to reveal the location of his smoked meats, which he had buried underground in the nearby thicket. The noose was carefully tightened, but at the last moment, they caught a whiff of a peach pie Margaret had placed in the kitchen window. He was released, and they enjoyed the southern delicacy. Three of his sons fought in the Battle of Stones River in Murfreesboro, only a few miles from their home, though they did not believe in slavery or secession. They were only interested in protecting their homes and families.

None of our family supported slavery. I am proud of that, but since they were on the losing side of the Conflict, they lost everything. There was, however, one member of the family who actually profited during those tumultuous years by selling rope to the Union. A bit of disloyalty in our family is condoned if it's in the interest of good business. No one epitomized this more than Sam Graham, my great-grandmother's uncle. He developed a successful farm in Hickman County, near Nashville, where he established one of the few plantations without slaves. At Pinewood, he developed a medieval township where his employees, though free, were encouraged to use the company store, company church, and company school. Any diversion from this established way of life was frowned upon and could lead to expulsion from the community. Rope was his bonanza, and he emerged from the war a wealthy man.

When the Civil War finally ended, he had the resources to send his son to Washington College in Virginia. The school suffered shortages of supplies, especially firewood. On one occasion, this shortage was exacerbated by someone stealing firewood from the headmaster's stack. Sam Graham's son decided to find the culprit. He bored the core out of one stick of firewood, filled it with gunpowder, and placed it back on the pile. A couple of nights later, a huge explosion blew the wing off a nearby home. No one was hurt, but he was summoned to the headmaster's office. After a short discussion, the headmaster, impressed with the boy's ingenuity, laughed it off and advised he use a little less powder next time.

Pinewood burned to the ground when I was in high school. Other than a few isolated photographs and a couch that sits in our front parlor, nothing remains, except that Petis Graham Gordon (my grandfather), Charles Graham Gordon (my father), Charles Graham Gordon, Jr. (my brother), and Graham Willis Gordon (my son), all bear witness in name to this amazing man.

Alfred White Gordon, John Hilton's son, moved out of the one-room log house and across the creek into what became the Old Home Place for future generations. Described as tall, slender, erect, and physically strong, he resembled the vast majority of Southerners at the time. He was quick tempered, and profanity was its fruit. Whenever he plowed the family garden, he asked his wife to take a chair and sit at the edge while he worked. This prohibited his cursing, since he respected her so much.

Like his father, he encountered trouble during the Civil War. He was escorted to the county courthouse, where he was ordered to sign an Oath of Allegiance to the Union. He refused. He later said that, although he opposed secession and supported the Union, he would never have signed an oath of allegiance because the repercussions of trying to explain it to his wife would have been far more severe than anything they could have done to him. His wife, Amanda Josephine Nelson Rosett, was as impressive as her name. She was drop-dead gorgeous. Her picture hangs above my desk, where she watches me and keeps any profanity in check.

Her son, James Petis Gordon, was a progressive farmer whose activities spanned from county commissioner who founded the county's first hospital, to state representative. His business successes accumulated three separate farms, one of which became my home today. Three months before his death at the age of eighty-six, he planted an eight-acre orchard, knowing he would never enjoy the fruit of his labor. He died before I was born, leaving his wife, Nettie Ann Jennings, to carry on alone.

She was my first memory. She sat in a wheelchair on the front porch of the home where I live today. I was five, and she was ninety-three. Her face is indistinguishable to me now, but I remember her hands folded over a shawl. Her twisted fingers were laced between one another like gnarled roots of an old Southern magnolia, her bony knuckles bursting above ground. She reached out and placed her hands on my head. I've always wondered what she was thinking, what she wanted to tell me. I wish I could remember her voice.

That is the genealogy, the video of the family vacation that no one cares about. As far as I am concerned, its only relevance is that it brought into existence the man who filled my world. By safely swimming to the shores of North Carolina in the late eighteenth century, Tommy Tatum set in motion a series of begets that resulted in seven generations of Gordons. Had any of them foreseen the coming of my grandfather, they would have gladly tossed aside all of their shortcomings and failures, considering their own lives complete and relevant because of their part in his existence.

CHAPTER TWO

The word grandfather positions a man somewhere in a family tree, somewhere in time. But my grandfather occupied more than a place or a time. He was actually a grand father. He stood in the gap where my father could not. No father can be all things to his children, so a grandfather helps shore up the foundation and patch up the weak areas. A grandfather is also able to enjoy the status of being grand because he has not inherited the responsibility of authority that falls to the father. Grandfathers get a free pass to respect and admiration, without the price paid for years of discipline allocated to fathers.

I called him by his initials, P.G. (Petis Graham). To address an elder in this way was generally perceived as disrespectful in our family, like calling my mother by her first name. I grew up calling everyone Mister or Miss or, in the case of relatives, Aunt Mildred or Cousin Margaret. But the initials P.G. were the highest form of praise and admiration, not unlike someone holding the distinction of VIP or PhD. His initials encompassed much more than the name Grandfather, Mr. Gordon, or Grandfather Gordon. These might appropriately fit some, but not my grandfather. So his initials represent respect, and are the *summa cum laude* of human nomenclature.

PG was the middle son of three boys. The oldest, Bob, was sent to the Webb School in Bell Buckle to obtain his education. The youngest, Henry, went to the Naval Academy in Annapolis, primarily because he could play baseball. PG was sickly, so he ended up on the front lines of Germany in WWI in a study-abroad program that may have proved to be more valuable than the stateside schools of his brothers. He once referenced Providence in a discussion we were having, so I asked him what he thought about God. He said on his voyage across the Atlantic to help the French he made a deal with God. PG did not elaborate on the finer points of the contract, but since he returned to the states three years later in one piece, God must have kept His end of the deal.

Though he rarely spoke of the Great War, he told me once that the happiest day of his life was November 11, 1918. A mud-filled trench had been his home for weeks, but the word went out that morning that they were going over the top. This phrase meant the boys were dragging themselves out of the trenches to march out into the open, where the odds of living were drastically reduced. Just before the word was given to move out, another messenger came running down the line yelling to hold on for another hour because the war had ended. So, on the eleventh hour of the eleventh day of the eleventh month, salvation came to my grandfather. It took him several months until he was shipped home, and he said he spent time in nearby bars talking to a variety of men, some of whom were the same Germans he was trying to kill earlier. As Thomas Hardy wrote, "Yes; quaint and curious war is! You shoot a fellow down you'd treat if met where any bar is, or help to half-a-crown."

When I visited PG as a child, I played with his old helmet and leggings, which were strewn in the corner of his shop. I put them on and marched out behind the house, where an old, abandoned rock-built chicken house stood. It reminded me of a bombed-out barrack, and I fought some major battles there. Then, called in for supper, I tossed his paraphernalia back in the same dank corner. It held little importance to him.

When he returned from Europe, he married Jessie Harrison, whom he had met at the Presbyterian Church at the end of Rock Springs Road. Some months later, they rendezvoused at the racetrack outside of Murfreesboro and eloped. Her father promised him a stake in his farm if PG worked for him for a predetermined amount of time, because his own son had left home. PG was in his third year of the contract when the prodigal returned. So, PG and his bride packed up their belongings and moved to a farm he thought he could afford, but the European education he had received in the French trenches gave him a peaceful satisfaction for any situation. He did not complain; he was, after all, alive. Perhaps contentment was the fine print in his contract with God.

Mocma, PG's wife and my grandmother, was born into money. Her father's horse dealership provided a life of ease for the Harrison household. She, however, had married into farming, the dignified poverty. Occasionally I spent the night with them, which was the only time I ever left home as a child. I heard him say to her one morning at the breakfast table that she didn't make biscuits like his mother. He said it with a smile, always showing his endearment in teasing ways. She immediately turned on her heels with a glare that startled me. Then she slowly and emphatically told him he didn't make dough like her father did. She didn't have quite the same expression, and she chuckled as she excused herself and walked away. It pleased him, nonetheless.

PG and my grandmother lived about six miles away from us in a community named Versailles. Although a French settlement, somewhere along the way the pronunciation grew phonetic. We pronounced it "For Sales." Founded in the eighteenth century as a trading post, it never knew prominence and existed as a languid, farming community, very much a Sleepy Hollow clone. Versailles actually thrived only as a suburb of the more important Rockvale, which we had no problem pronouncing; neither did we misunderstand the origin of its name. PG's farm was rock on rock at the base of a knob. Somehow, he eked out a living milking cows by hand. He also spent a lot of his time at our farm, leaving Mocma alone for most of the day. She often referred to our home as The Holy Land. The inflection of her voice lacked any measure of endearment. I felt the tension from PG as he tried to appease her while keeping up with the daily workings of both farms. I loved my grandmother, but her intensity at times strained PG's attempts at making her happy to the point of his resignation, and he came to our home for a short, daily vacation.

My grandfather walked everywhere. His long, narrow frame floated like a ribbon in the wind as he paced through an alfalfa field or kicked clods in a freshly plowed plot. Every step told him something. Shades of green indicated plant health, and he could make a spontaneous prognosis that professional soil tests later confirmed. He'd stoop down and run his fingers through crimson clover, his hand acting as a comb, much like the way he caressed my grandmother's hair. In early spring he'd pick up a handful of soil, let it crumble between his fingers, and tell us exactly when to start plowing. He was rarely wrong. Soil is finicky, like my grandmother, and he knew when to work it and when to leave it alone. "If you work the dirt when it's too wet, it balls up in hard clods that makes mean goings," he would say. I witnessed PG using the wrong words at the wrong time to my grandmother, and she would turn into a hard clod that took days of mean goings to soften.

Sometimes he strolled peacefully across the farm, not necessarily in search of knowledge but for the sheer joy of it. With head bowed, arms behind him, hands clasped, he walked a short distance, stopped, looked around as if he'd lost something, then resumed his slow and deliberate gait. He was never in a hurry, and, on those occasions when I walked with him, I regarded him as some great American who was also my friend. Gordon men treat communication like a job, using it only if necessary to accomplish some tangible goal. The women understand that the finer point of communication is conversation, something beautiful, relational, and intangible. So neither of us said much; it was just a pleasure being in his presence. And so he paced across the land he loved, never dreaming of treating it with any less respect than his own family.

Farming was changing, though. The horses and mules had disappeared from the farming landscape, and farming practices were reflecting the shift from agriculture to agribusiness. Culture is an art form involving the unseen elements of humanity. Business is more calculated, negating the effect of the spirit. Manure was replaced with synthetic fertilizers. Diversity of crops turned into monoculture. The knowledge of how to outsmart pests was traded for insecticides and, with the migration of the newest generation to the city, the family farm grew larger to maximize efficiency. My grandfather was being ushered into a time in which he felt alien.

When herbicides and chemical fertilizers appeared, he was apprehensive, but even this patron of the old order smiled rather sheepishly when corn yields increased with few apparent problems. He watched my father stir chemicals with his bare hands in a homemade fifty-five-gallon spray apparatus. The chalky herbicide left a residue all over his clothes and body. As herbicides improved, we used some chemicals that had to be disked into the soil immediately after application. So we drove directly behind the sprayer, inhaling the fumes. I vividly remember spending an entire day disking behind my father as he applied the herbicide. That evening my eyes twitched deep into the night, and the smell remained in my nose for days.

The success took us all by surprise. No weeds, no damaging insects, high yields. The idea that we could plant a crop of corn and not be concerned about plowing out the weeds was mind-boggling. Before herbidices, we planted fifty acres of corn, and then the rain set in for a week or so. The corn shot up, but so too did the weeds, and before the ground dried out enough to plow the center of the rows out, the crop was lost. But that was then. Now the chemicals made the cultivator obsolete. Insects took a back seat to this revolution as well. It was all too easy. Years later, when my father and some of his contemporaries were dying of Parkinson's Disease, which had been linked by some to the use of these chemicals, my grandfather continued to stroll across his fields. We wondered if the cost of high yields had been too great. Even now, forty years later, after a long day's work my hand has a slight tremor, and I wonder what it has cost me.

In late August, silage-chopping season began. Even now, I can feel autumn approaching and remember the smells of corn silage. The entire corn plant was chopped into small pieces, taken by wagons to the silo and blown sixty feet in the air through a chute into the interior where it began the fermentation process. Much like taking a cucumber and converting it to a sweet pickle, the corn was transformed into the pleasant aroma of silage. The silos were sixty feet tall, composed of concrete staves held together by metal bands three feet apart. We thought nothing of climbing the outside to get to the top. To climb, we had to place our foot on one ring and reach up to the next one. When I was young I could barely reach one to the other, but it never dawned on any of us that falling was an option. It was rock climbing without the ropes.

One summer before entering high school, I read Homer's *Odyssey* while pulling wagons back and forth from the field to the silos on our Massey Ferguson-35 tractor. Each day was a new adventure. I was Odysseus in journeying far down Rock Springs Road, where I hooked up to a silage wagon, then hauled it back to Ithaca. Each trek was twenty years. Crossing the bridge, I imagined the Sirens with their seductive lure in the creek. Driving past the huge sinkhole we used for a trash dump, I saw Charybdis sucking in the world. Unloading the silage into the blower was feeding Polyphemus the Cyclops. The sound of the straining tractor echoed his roar. Imagination changed everything, and the day tripped by.

At certain times of the year between crops a lull provided time for more leisurely activities. PG and I took full advantage by grabbing our fishing poles and heading off to the creek. We would drive back to the north forty, where a small creek meandered through rocky pastures suitable only for grazing cattle. We set the minnow trap in a shallow pool with stale bread crumbs inside. Within a few hours, we had a cage full of minnows that we took back to the deepest part of the creek where the bass hung out under the weeping willow. We took the live minnows and pierced them with a hook just below the top fin so they continued to wiggle underwater to lure the bass. Then we waited.

Sitting on the bank of Dry Fork with my grandfather anchored me. On the opposite bank, where the huge willow tree bowed gracefully and beautifully above the ground, its massive root system underground held the soil in the bend of the creek and protected the bank from erosion. I often sat and watched the reflection of that willow in the water as it coincided with the reflection of my grandfather on the opposite side. Just as the willow protected the soil from the ravages of heavy rains, he protected me from the emotional floods that often came my way. He was that tree planted by the stream.

Some days he lit his pipe, drew in heavily, and advised me not to smoke. I can still see him pulling out his Prince Albert tobacco, packing it ever so gently in his pipe, then lighting it with his silver-plated lighter. The flame drew up and down as he inhaled, and the aroma provided the perfect backdrop for our fishing experience. He started smoking as a youngster, when he was plagued with asthma. The doctor, his uncle, recommended smoking, which must have worked since he never seemed short of breath. Sometimes we fished for hours with no fish to show for our efforts. Then he reeled in his bait, smiled, and remarked how much fun it had been.

It was on the banks of Dry Fork that I received a unique education. He taught me that if a snapping turtle bit me, it wouldn't let go until it thundered. We occasionally caught a snapper on our lines and, when we pulled it to the bank, PG killed it and hung it on a nearby fence as a reminder to other snappers the consequences of stealing our minnows. If on occasion I complained about something that seemed unfair, he responded with, "Don't let those stud ducks turn you around." That was all. Often when I asked him what of two decisions he would make in the hypothetical scenario I proposed, he simply nodded. Sometimes his French education slipped out, and he coaxed the fish with a whispered, "Beaucoup, beaucoup." His demeanor exuded patience, gentleness, and kindness. Without saying it, he taught me that fishing had little to do with fish. I can still clearly hear my grandfather's voice. It ripples through my mind, bobbing with inflection and love, like the afternoons we spent on Dry Fork.

Years later, when our children were young, I dug a pond beside our home and stocked it with channel catfish. I wanted to sit on its bank and fish with them. I wanted to light a pipe and tell my kids never to smoke. I wanted to say nothing at all, to speak to them without words of how much I enjoyed being with them. I wanted to tell them about snapping turtles, but above all, I wanted them to know my voice. Unfortunately, the pond leaked after a couple of years. Despite all our efforts, it dried up each summer.

I could not recreate those happy, spontaneous moments of my childhood. It was like catching a glimpse of something out of the corner of my eye in a dark room, but when I turned to look, it had disappeared. Dry Fork still flows to the Stones River. The rocks we sat on while fishing are still embedded there, and the man who sanctified the place remains in my periphery where he belongs, and I hope that, in some way, in my children's periphery, I have sanctified some place or part of their lives.

PG had a couple of girlfriends, in addition to his wife. One was an MT John Deere tricycle-wheeled tractor with a sickle mower attachment. It had a small seat beside the main one where I rode for hours beside him as he cut hay or clipped pastures. He and that tractor had spent a lot of time together since replacing the mules, and their relationship was solid. To see alfalfa falling in synchronized fashion over the mower, the occasional rabbit darting out of its way, the sound of the mower itself with its scissor-like clippity clippity, leaning half asleep against my grandfather on a warm June day was as good as life could be at ten years old. Like being rocked to sleep by a male counterpart of my mother, he cradled me. But at the same time, we were still engaged in a manly endeavor. It was still machine and smoke, and it was important. We were farming together.

His other, and more important, mistress was Della May, a sleek piece of craftsmanship. When he put his hands on her, the ecstasy in his eyes was clear. Her front end was narrow and exquisite, but it was her backside that everyone talked about. More than seven feet wide with narrow tires, she had a low center of gravity that modern tractors only dream of. She was a Farmall from the 1930s. Her workload had diminished with the addition of larger and more efficient tractors, so PG only used her sparingly for pulling rocks out of fields. He had dated her for decades, and the two were as one. I was fortunate enough to use her on rare occasions for disking fields.

Della May was older than electrical ignitions, and she had to be started using a hand crank on the front end. Just as you ran the risk of being kicked by hooking up a mule from the backside, cranking Della May from the front was even more dangerous. When she started, if the crank was not removed quickly, she recoiled, and the crank became a weapon. Even the most experienced farmers sometimes ended up with a broken arm. I was never strong enough, so my father cranked it for me and then sent me to the field.

Della May's seat was supported by a large spring that acted like a shock absorber, giving me a soft up and down motion, resembling that of a gaited horse or a jumper seen in the Olympics. But when I arrived in the field to start disking, she transformed into a thoroughbred. We disked around and around the field, and the synchronized up-and-down motion took us to prominent race-tracks around the country. She and I won numerous Kentucky Derbies. In one day alone, we won the Triple Crown. She would have given Secretariat a run for the roses. Then we returned to the shed, where I backed her into her stall until another day. We finally retired her and donated her to a museum. I visit her from time to time to rehash some of our most impressive victories. I had a special relationship with Della May, but PG was always her first love.

Apart from farming, PG and Mocma also raised a family. They had five children, but two died in infancy, which was not uncommon in that day. Of those who survived, the eldest was Aunt Guy. She possessed the unique combination of a comical and no-nonsense persona. On certain occasions, her expression sparked a fearful dread, then, only moments later, she'd laugh out loud. She was painfully frank, and had little time for small talk. She understood tragedy. Two of her children suffered from diabetes. In those days the treatment was guesswork, so she struggled with daily doses of insulin, never knowing how it affected her children. She buried both of them as adults. She outlived her husband, a kind and quiet man, and in her last days watched her daughter-in-law succumb to cancer, leaving her son, Pettus, to care for her, which he did faithfully. But she was a fighter and continued to fondly harass the nurses in the nursing home with her stony expression. But like all of us, they saw beneath the surface of this remarkable woman and loved her intensely.

Her sister, Aunt Lou, wore a face of pure delight. Every word spoken was accompanied with a smile or laughter. Her husband,

Uncle Jug, exuded the same optimism, which came in handy as a traveling salesman. I asked him once how he and Aunt Lou enjoyed such a wonderful relationship since he was absent from home so often. "That's the secret," he said with a smile. They raised two boys. The younger one, Bubba, was closer to my age, and I loved him like a brother. He earned an architectural degree and worked in Nashville. One night, after working early into the morning, Bubba went to his car to go home. A young man approached him, demanded money, then shot and killed him. Bubba left behind a pregnant wife and two children.

The evening of his death, several family members gathered at PG's home to break the news. At this time, technology had not progressed to the point of prohibiting the sharing of grief face to face. He was sitting in his favorite recliner as we pulled chairs up around him in a semi-circle. Mocma had died several years before, so PG lived alone. He wrote letters to her each evening, just to let her know what he had been doing and how much he missed her. So we came that night to deliver the bad news. Gordons aren't known for their tact, so the first born, Aunt Guy, lead the charge and blurted, "Daddy, Bubba was killed last night." No details were necessary and, without hesitation, PG quietly moaned, "Oh, Uncle Alf."

I was sitting next to him, and I was completely taken off guard because Uncle Alf had died fifty years before, but PG told me many times how much he loved his uncle and what a shock it was when he suddenly died in his mid-fifties. Now, fifty years later, the hurt and loss of his uncle welled up inside like hot magma and spewed forth this old pain with one mighty eruption. He had to get Uncle Alf out to make room for this new tragedy. There was not enough room for them both. Lowering his chin upon his cane, he stared straight ahead without tears. Then, turning his head slowly to the side, he looked at the empty chair where his wife had sat for more than sixty years, and it seemed to me he found that slim silver lining. At least she was spared the horror of it all. Consoling a man who had seen so much in ninety years seemed superfluous, so my father and I shook his hand and left.

When PG turned ninety-four, he was invited to attend a Middle Tennessee State University halftime football game as only one of two remaining WWI veterans in Rutherford County. My brother and I escorted him there. First, they introduced the Vietnam veterans and the crowd applauded, then the Korean War and WWII veterans received increased enthusiasm. Finally, my grandfather and his comrade were introduced, and I was astounded as the entire crowd rose to its feet with a deafening roar. My grandfather took it all in without emotion. I bent down to his wheelchair and asked what he thought about it. "It's okay," he said without inflection. His response immediately took me back to an interview I had done with him while I was in middle school concerning Alvin York, the WWI Tennessee hero. I asked PG what this hero meant to him. "Not much," he said, with that same lack of emotion. He went on to say that Alvin York hadn't done anything more than all the other boys who died trying. It didn't enhance my report, but I learned that my grandfather did not make a habit of building pedestals.

A few years, later he went to the hospital for a check-up. The doctor wasn't comfortable with his findings, so ordered more testing and sent him to the nursing home next door for a brief stay. PG calmly said he wasn't going to stay there. My mother agreed and told him that as soon as he regained his strength he would return to his home in Versailles. He reiterated that he wasn't going to stay. They moved him over peacefully. Later that evening my mother went by to check on him. He was dead. We then understood what he meant.

I received the news that evening. My legs buckled, and I collapsed onto the couch. I had not seen him that day; I had not said goodbye. I did not know what to do, and I felt so alone. He represented so much of what was good in my childhood. He was my only witness when I caught a five-pound bass out of Dry Fork. We cut hay together, spent nights together, ate grapefruit and fig newton bars for breakfast, walked in silence together, rode together in his old pickup, and now he had moved on, without me.

I hated seeing him in the coffin. Some look natural in the reclining position, but PG wasn't a horizontal type of man. Although I don't remember anyone accusing him of being handsome, dressed up as he was in the coffin he was rather dapper. Lying there, he reminded me of the nights I spent with him. In the middle of the night, he would often scream. At first, I thought nightmares from the Great War haunted him, but later I learned it was leg cramps. Mocma got up and rubbed his bulging calves until the knots diminished and then disappeared altogether. Then he lay down to a peaceful sleep while she and I waited for the next round. Sometimes it happened several times in a night.

At length, the lid of the casket was closed, the service concluded, and we all made the ten-mile trek to the Gordon cemetery where he was placed beside his wife. No cramps to disturb either of them. The foot marker paid tribute to his service in WWI as a bugler. It was a blustery day in October, and the maple trees were turning. My father, who was in the last years of losing a battle with Parkinson's Disease, slumped quietly in his wheelchair as the preacher said a few appropriate words. He concluded with something about the resurrection of the dead, but it seemed too distant to matter to me then.

Built on the highest part of the farm, the cemetery gave a panoramic view of the land my grandfather loved so much. I gazed up at the giant cedars that had seen Gordon after Gordon planted beneath them. They swayed gently with quiet resignation. PG was lowered, covered, and that was that. The men made their way to the fence overlooking the fields. Farmers, and country people in general, are more at peace leaning on a fence while discussing life, death, and the price of this year's corn crop. In time, everyone slowly filed away. We were the last to leave. I don't know how much he comprehended, but my father's face was moist with tears. We then wheeled Daddy out of the cemetery, leaving PG to catch up with family.

My grandfather survived a World War, the deaths of two children, the murder of a grandson, the drowning of another, the death of his wife and all of his siblings, and he witnessed his only son's twelve-year demise to disease. Yet he never lost his light-hearted, joyful countenance. He grieved alone in his own way and never allowed his pain to burden others. It was always well with his soul.

I think of him each fall when the maple trees turn. Their spectacular hues remind me of the colorful man who filled my world, each leaf representing a memory: strolling over the farm with his hands strategically positioned behind him, the smell of Prince Albert tobacco as he slowly inhaled, the loving affection he had for his wife, the stories, the soothing smile, and—best of all—fishing off the bank of Dry Fork, anchored by the roots of this great man.

CHAPTER THREE

I called him Daddy from as early as I can remember. I never used the word father unless telling others about him. My father was a successful farmer. My father was handsome and amazingly athletic. My father was greatly respected in the community. My father was the man I wanted to emulate. I was so proud to be his son. But it was my daddy who brought me a wristwatch one afternoon for no reason, my daddy who didn't whip me when I broke his pool cue, my daddy who took me to a state football final game to see my first cousin play, and my daddy who provided a way for me to attend a private boys' school, which had a big impact on my life.

I never understood my father. I wasn't aware that he could be understood, and I certainly never considered taking the time to get to know him better. Fathers are not to be known. They just do what they do, with little fanfare. There was no doubt that our father was head of the family, although he never said so. He simply had a presence, and we were all awestruck. Great leaders never have to define their authority. But one afternoon I saw a different side of my father, a side that perplexed and even frightened me because he seemed too human, too frail to be the man I put on the pedestal, and it happened on just another normal day on the farm.

The boar weighed in at 400 pounds. He stood in a large stall, one that was made considerably smaller by his presence. With an arched back and mastodon tusks rising from either side of his jaws, he resembled something out of Greek myth. Coarse, shiny black hair hung down around his massive body. Shadows in the stall made it difficult to anticipate his movement, as he appeared to float about his confinement. He strode around with a regal confidence, making the bold statement he was no ordinary pig but fell into the higher class of porcine called swine.

While the hired hand, along with my brother and me, gazed on in mortal fear, my father approached from behind and asked if we were ready. It wasn't a question. He never asked questions and he never waited for answers. They were obvious and imperative. The task before us was to catch the boar, throw him to the ground, and hold him long enough for my father to cut the tusks out. The removal of tusks prevented any damage to other pigs and to us, in that order.

Entering this small amphitheater brought to mind stories of gladiators. We managed to wrestle him to the ground. It was July, and the dust boiled out of the pen as we struggled to keep him flat on the ground, difficult to do with an animal shaped like a watermelon. Three of us penned him when my father approached the boar's head to do the surgery. To our surprise, he approached, not with a saw or clippers but with a hammer. We looked at each other with the same fear the boar's eyes held just moments before. The psychological edge we had over the boar evaporated and, for the sake of self-preservation, our fingers dug deeply into his callous hide.

My father locked the door behind him. There was no way out. When the hammer struck the tusk, the boar erupted like a volcano. His huge head writhed and foam shot out and sprayed us with a frothy mist. Although we outweighed him, he had a decided advantage with the onset of the hammer. Adrenalin and fury surged in repeated convoluted twists of his huge body, but by bolting the door my father gave us a newfound source of power to survive. If the boar got to his feet, we faced sure destruction. The hammer continued to find its mark, and the sounds of men cursing and the high-pitched squeal of a mad boar boiled out with the dust. Each swing of the hammer pained my father greatly, but in a curious anger, he pounded away. Finally, after what seemed like forever, the tusks were extracted. We released the boar and dashed for the door, but it was unnecessary as he was slow to rise. He just stood there, bleeding through his mouth, broken. If a woman's glory is her hair, a boar's must be his tusks, and we had effectively emasculated him from the anterior end.

That evening, returning home from milking, I noticed my father standing at the doorway of the shed looking in at the boar. Generally, my father's posture exuded pride and an optimism common to his generation, but as this evening gave way to night, he stood slumped, head down, talking to the boar. I paused and wondered what common ground the two had in eliciting such a clandestine meeting. They were both powerhouses of their species. As a boar, my father would have been a blue ribbon winner at the state fair. So, too, would this boar. Before he lost his tusks, that is, and perhaps that is what my father saw.

Growing up, I heard many stories about my father's athletic prowess. Adolph Rupp, legendary coach of the University of Kentucky, came to see him play basketball at Rockvale High School the year Daddy took them to the state tournament. Rupp offered him a scholarship. Declining the invitation, he, instead, enrolled at a junior college where he played football, baseball, and basketball, and was voted greatest athlete at the school. Later he was inducted into their Hall of Fame. Everyone said he could have played professional baseball, but when the scouts came to Rockvale recruiting talent, he remained at home plowing the soil in preparation for spring planting. Once he hit a baseball over the school's gymnasium during a Fourth of July celebration. No one had ever done it before, and no one ever did it again. It measured about five hundred feet. In the military during WWII, he set a record on an obstacle course somewhere in Georgia. It held for decades. Later in life, he worked for the VA hospital helping veterans regain their confidence through sports. At one point, he taught them how to bowl, a game he had never played. Within a few months, he bowled back-to-back perfect games.

During those early years, he became the admiration of a small town. He grew mighty tusks. But as he aged, there were regrets of not attending the University of Kentucky, not trying out for the professional baseball team, not growing even larger tusks. He told me once that the greatest time of his life was in college. "I was somebody then," I still remember him saying as he stared into the distance. His father repeatedly told him to return to the farm where he could make a decent living and keep the farm in the family. He was, after all, the only son and heir to the sacred soil. As nurturing as my grandfather was to me, in his relationship to his son, my father, there existed a noticeable gap.

So he gave up sports and returned to the farm, back to the proverbial small, dusty shed where his tusks were systematically removed forever. Sadly, when a young man's life peaks at an early age and his value is based upon transient talents and gifts, the remainder of his life, as he is overlooked, is the slow dying of candlelight. The wick disappears, and his tusks are removed forever. The pain is excruciating, and well my father knew as he stood at the doorway gazing at the boar that evening.

A part of me envied that boar. I longed to have my father stand at the doorway of my room talking to me, telling me about his dreams and disappointments. Sharing himself with me would have eliminated much of my speculation about him now. It is difficult only to surmise about the one who gave me his eyes, his long narrow face, and his curly blonde hair. It is empty to look into a mirror and see only the physical attributes, wondering at all the rest.

My father suffered greatly at the hands of a debilitating disease for twelve years. He couldn't communicate well by the time he went to the nursing home where he spent the final three years of his life. I visited a day or two each week, giving my mother a break from the relentless task of caregiving. I fed him, cleaned mucous from his mouth, wiped his forehead with a damp cloth, and sat beside him waiting for something. It was like sitting on the banks on Dry Fork, except the creek was dry, and I hopelessly waited for anything. I was not accustomed to sitting alone with this man as I had with my grandfather. I wanted to talk to Daddy, but I did not know what to say. We had not practiced much over the years. He was my hero, but I had learned that heroes are more heroic at a distance. So, after a time, I rose, held his hand, and said goodbye. He made no response, at least nothing I detected.

This went on for a couple of years, and then one day after going through our regular routine, I again said goodbye, and, as I walked out of the room, I heard him say, "I love you." I was thirty-three years old, and I had never heard those words addressed to me from him. He had said them in many tangible ways, but not the words themselves. I turned around in the doorway of his room, unable to leave or return. I just stood there. Then slowly I said, "I love you, too, Daddy." Then I did something I have and perhaps never will understand. I just walked out of the room and returned home. I never discussed it with him again.

I have relived that moment many times. I see myself walking back into the room, kissing him on the forehead, sitting beside him, telling him why he was important to me. I had a chance to tell him that I loved him with or without tusks, but I didn't. Thoughtlessly I hammered away and left him alone in his dusty shed. I did not know him or myself well enough to understand how similar we were. I possessed much of his looks, but it would take years to discover the hidden gems of his character that I now try to emulate.

The boar eventually recovered and, even without his tusks, fathered a crop of piglets from his harem. I doubt if any of his sows thought any less of him. There is much to glean from that old boar: How being male has its challenges; How we learn, sooner or later, that we are not loved or admired for our ability to strut about maintaining our macho image with our mighty tusks. We realize how quickly these tusks fade away. When the pride of life finally gives way, we find ourselves surprised it was never the tusks that were the attraction. We are ultimately valued for our ability to love those closest to us in ordinary ways.

I felt guilty for the pain that boar suffered on that hot summer day. So much so, that as I prepared for bed that night, I developed a mild toothache. The sounds of the hammer banging relentlessly against the tusks echoed in my bedroom and made their way to my tooth. I thought of asking my father's advice on relieving the pain of a toothache, but refrained in light of the day's activities. No, asking my mother was a better plan. She was the nurturer in the family, but, more importantly, she lacked experience with a hammer.

CHAPTER
FOUR

My mother was a rebel. Her heart was wild and free. She threw off the accepted norm that rebels always stand out and march to a different drummer. She lived ninety-two rebellious years in the guise of a traditional housewife and mother, but all the while her undercover work proceeded unabated as she embodied her past, stamping an image on all who took the time to know her. But I'm getting ahead of myself. When she was seventy, she wrote her autobiography and called it *Just Me*. In it, she gave a vivid account of the years from her birth to marriage. It is filled with honesty. No philosophy, no moral lessons, no hidden agenda. It was just her.

Because my mother always lived in the present, she remembered the past acutely, but because she lived fully in the present, the past held little importance. Rebels never look back.

Catherine Bateman Hartman descended from the Buchanan line, who emigrated from Ireland in the 1700s. According to a number of historical documents (the ones we prefer), John Buchanan, Sr. came to Nashville before James Robertson, the traditional founder of Nashville. I doubt if John was waiting on the banks of the Cumberland River waving to James, but there is some indication he was there. His son, Major John Buchanan, Jr. joined with John Donelson, the other co-founder of Nashville. John Buchanan Jr. was engaged in defending the colonists from Indian attacks. His father died in one of these attacks, and his mother witnessed her husband's scalping. Just as a side note, my wife's fourth great-grandfather was there as well and signed the Cumberland Compact, Nashville's first Constitution, so our ancestors knew each other. Mine were outside the fort being scalped; hers were inside doing the paperwork. Anyway, John Buchanan, Jr. also served in the Revolutionary War and the War of 1812, but his greatest claim to fame was his descendent- Mary Kate Patterson Davis Hill Kyle, my mother's great-great aunt.

Aunt Kate was one of the most famous female spies of the Civil War. She used her good looks and charm to carry important information across Union lines. When Sam Davis was caught and hanged in Columbia, Tennessee, it was Kate who went there, identified the body, and returned him to his home in Smyrna, which is today a historical landmark. No historian will verify her claim, but

I prefer folklore to truth any day. She later married Sam's brother, who was the first of her three husbands. She outlived them all.

Amazing as it may seem, my mother knew this Civil War heroine. She died when my mother was only nine years old, but, in keeping with Momma's remarkable memory, she remembered Aunt Kate well. What a passing of the torch it must have been when they met. There are so many legends about this lady that I am forced to believe them all. She carried loaded pistols under her petticoat well into her eighties. Near the end of her life, she reportedly slept under her house in fear of Union soldiers. When she died in 1931 at the age of ninety-three, she was buried in Confederate Circle in Mount Olivet Cemetery in Nashville, the only woman so honored.

Aunt Kate's great nephew was Paul Hartman, my grandfather. I never knew him as he died when my mother was only fifteen. His wife, who I called Grandmother, was bigger than life. At birth, she weighed only a pound. She was so small her entire face could be covered with a silver dollar. No one gave her any chance, but rebels always defy conventional knowledge. She had to be turned on the hour to keep her head from becoming too flat. She survived, made up for lost time, and topped the scales, exceeding two hundred pounds before she died.

Grandmother's amazing talent for playing the piano exceeded her weight. I used to watch her fingers move across the keys effortlessly, producing the most amazing sounds. She never took a lesson, but she bade all eighty-eight keys to do her will. Her triceps had been converted to baggy, hanging skin that churned like pistons when she hunkered down. She once wrote a song, *Boogey-Woogey*, which was fast, furious, and inspiring, not to be played in church.

It was her way of letting it all out, breaking free, rebelling. No one ever taped it, but I remember it resembled something like deep soul jazz.

When I was in middle school, I played junior pro football. Each afternoon I took the bus to her house after school. She always had a little sweet treat for me, and I watched *Gomer Pyle*. Her mother, Nanny, lived in the adjoining room. Every afternoon Nanny played solitaire, and Grandmother often told me that she had never lost a game. Then she added, "Cheats every time." At 4 o'clock, she drove me to football practice in her old Chevrolet Biscayne. Words were few as we drove to the field each day, but I was comfortable with her. She wasn't the overly affectionate type of grandmother, but I knew she loved me. After she died, I acquired the Biscayne and drove it during my four years of college. No one thought it would run that long, but, like Grandmother, it endured.

Grandmother was part German, and in keeping with that history she suffered loss often. In April of 1930, in the midst of the Great Depression, her house burned. She, her husband, and four children lost everything. In April of 1937, she lost her husband, so she raised three girls and a handicapped son by herself. To feed her family, she taught in a one-room school. She had the first hot-lunch program in the county simply by heating the potbellied stove early in the morning. When the students arrived, they put their canned goods in a pot of water on the stove. By lunchtime, the meal was ready. This simple, practical approach to challenges also helped her survive as a widow and mother, although perhaps she was also helped by rebel stubbornness. She beat the odds. Like Aunt Kate,

Grandmother married multiple times and outlived them all. Her children, who were her greatest legacy, inherited her resolve.

Aunt Helen, her oldest daughter, worshipped her family's genealogy. She belonged to Americans of Royal Descent, Huguenot Founders of Virginia, First Families of Tennessee, Daughters of the American Revolution, Daughters of the War of 1812, and Daughters of the Civil War. She had authentic documents and shiny brooches to prove all of her memberships. Momma joined them also, not so much for the history but because she loved to be with people, the living ones. She was not impressed with those who couldn't converse. Momma often said, "When the horse is dead, get off." Aunt Helen, on the other hand, loved her ancestry with a marked pride and rode that dead horse most of her life. She was also a perfectionist in many areas, but none more than her expertise of the English language. She could diagram a sentence while in conversation. My (adjective) Aunt Helen (proper noun/subject) loved (transitive verb) the (article) English language (direct object) and (conjunction) those (direct object/pronoun) who (relative pronoun) spoke (verb) it (pronoun) well (adverb). She loved the rest of us, too.

She, a literary rebel, loathed new politically correct words being added to the dictionary, and she came to pieces at the use of the word *hopelessly*. I have no idea why, but it had something to do with the misuse of an adverb, or perhaps she subconsciously deplored the thought of anything being hopeless; she was, after all, a Hartman. Aunt Helen was beautiful, and the love she received from her husband perpetuated that beauty. Her soft countenance exposed her kind and reserved nature, but there was that element of mystery in her protected laugh that made one think she was on the verge of actually enjoying herself, but not quite. I was fortunate to know her in her twilight years when the colors are truest.

Aunt Claire, the youngest of the three girls, was not as proper as Aunt Helen, making her funnier and more enjoyable. Her life was made more difficult by her husband's drinking, so she never really cared much about her ancestors who protected the colonists. It was all she could do to keep her own scalp. Life with an alcoholic drained her natural beauty, except her eyes that always had a special sparkle to them. Her wit was dry as dust, and her deadpan expression made her humor hysterical. She raised two children, and she persevered, as was the custom of the Hartman girls. She died before I had time to really know her as a person, other than just being my aunt.

The youngest member of the family was their little brother, Paul. We called him Buster for reasons I do not know. He had rheumatoid arthritis as a child and was partially paralyzed throughout his body He was only four feet tall and walked with a slow, painful shift. He could not turn his head from side to side, and I pitied him. He was loved and cared for by his sisters and, when he died at the age of forty-three, we were grieved but also relieved. He had suffered so much.

The three girls sang together and were often compared to the Andrews Sisters. They sang on the radio, in church, and at funerals and weddings. Aunt Helen's soprano voice dominated, while Aunt Claire's baritone (she smoked) gave the trio its anchor. My mother's alto brought it all together. Momma's father was the song leader for many churches, depending on the need of any particular Sunday.

Momma attributed her love for music to him. He died when she was only fifteen. She always spoke fondly of him, so I was caught off guard one Sunday morning while visiting her at the nursing home.

Our conversation lagged, and she looked away from me and said abruptly, "I suppose you know that my daddy cheated on my mother." She said it in such a matter-of-fact tone that I thought I must have misunderstood, so I sat awkwardly still. I could hardly breathe and hoped I heard incorrectly. She continued, "I remember the Saturday afternoon when he got all dressed up, shined his shoes, combed back his hair, and drove away to see another woman. When he drove out of the driveway, my mother went to a corner of the den, cuddled up on the floor, and cried. I sat beside her for a long time." She stopped and took a long look at me as if she had forgotten I was there. "I don't know why I told you that." With that, the conversation ended. We sat in silence until at length I said, "I am so sorry, Momma." She didn't say anything else, and we never spoke of it again. Usually when she told me of difficult times in her life, which was rare, she always concluded with a "Not to worry" or a "This too shall pass." But this time was different. She had worried, and it had not passed for more than seventy-five years.

Momma had a strong faith, not so much in words but in lifestyle. She never forced her beliefs on me, but her manner of living eventually attracted me to Christ. She didn't talk about Him much, but I sensed she talked to Him often. I don't remember her praying aloud publicly, which I respected greatly. Most prayers are either sermons directed toward someone, informational treatises to God of things He already knows, or ways of using spiritual vocabulary that God Himself might have trouble understanding. Momma said a lot more with a bowed head. She taught me a lot about the book of Proverbs, and even today when I read them, I hear her voice, not Solomon's. She had a unique way of combining her faith with the tangible world that made everything real, and Monday morning was no less sacred than Sunday.

One year I tried out for a baseball team to make my father proud. On the day of the tryouts, the coaches positioned themselves to get a good look at the talent so they could divide up among themselves the players into teams, trying to keep them equal. I was sent to the outfield to catch a few fly balls. The coach hit one right to me. I put the glove in front of my face, but the ball came in a little higher than I thought. It grazed the top of my glove and hit me dead on the forehead. I waved away any help, took two steps, and collapsed. I can still imagine the coaches looking at each other thinking, *Nope, not this one.*

That was one of my better days. As a left-handed batter, I was hit many times by pitches. The pitchers just could not get used to my being on the wrong side of the plate, which as it turned out was the only way I ever got on base. After a half season of this brutality, I told Momma one evening that I was going to quit. She was setting the table for supper, and without looking up and without any emotion, she said, "You can't quit." It was not like her to be so dogmatic, so I asked why. She said that if I quit, I would be a quitter, and we didn't do that sort of thing. That was all she said and, since her words were backed by her life, I finished the season with more than my share of bruises but a sense of accomplishment. At least I wasn't a quitter. She had an amazing way of moving me with such little effort.

Growing up on our farm was hectic. Momma worked constantly and had little time to sit down and enjoy a conversation. So, when I needed to talk to her about something important, I went to the edge of the stove where she prepared meals and I unloaded my troubles. When I finished, she stopped for an instant, looked me straight in the eyes, and said something that had nothing to do with what I said but everything to do with what I meant. She listened to my heart, and when she did this, she said she loved me at the deepest level. She pondered, not in her mind, like most of us do. Her heart had an intellect of its own.

My mother gave me a love for learning. Never an avid reader, what I did read was from her insistence on having many books in our home. I was never assigned books to read, but they were always available, and eventually I began picking them up for enjoyment. She appeared to enjoy learning about everything. If I was interested in space travel, she was too, and she bought me space books. When I wrote a speech for 4-H on the subject of dairy farming, she came up with the opening line, "When was milk the highest? When the cow jumped over the moon." Regardless of my interest, she expressed the same thrill and kept me reaching for stars with determination and expectation.

Momma made Christmas. Her enthusiasm was contagious. In search of a Christmas tree, we walked miles to find the perfect specimen. Normally, details evaded her, but when it came to the Christmas tree, she was relentless. Finally, we dragged the long sought-after prize back to the house, secured it in the stand, and placed it in the living room where she began the arduous task of decorating it with an infinite number of icicles. It turned into a masterpiece. She and Daddy always made Christmas special. After the morning milking was completed, we gathered at the living room door, youngest first. The door was opened, and we ran in to see what Santa had brought. I don't remember the gifts, but I can't forget her attitude. She loved it as much as we did. It was wonderful having a happy mother, a funny mother, a loving mother, and she was all of these on Christmas day.

After graduating from Webb School, I took it upon myself to write to the board of directors requesting that the Headmaster be removed because he did not reflect the major tenets of the school (eighteen years old, and I knew it all). When I finished writing the letter, I gave it to my mother for her editorial advice and endorsement. I fully expected her to explain that it could be hurtful to others and counsel me not to send it. Instead, she said that I should send it. I looked at her inquisitively, but if I had considered Aunt Kate, it made sense. Momma explained that when you believe strongly in something, you should see it through, regardless of the outcome. "There are no lost causes," she often said.

Momma possessed a plethora of hobbies. *Plethora* is the word she taught me while playing Scrabble. It means abundance. I would have used abundance, but plethora is the word she would have used to beat me. Besides her love for words, another hobby was playing pranks on unsuspecting victims. Once, I took her to the annual Farm Bureau dinner meeting. We arrived early, got our food, and sat down near the front where the speakers gave their addresses. We finished our meal, and the meeting began with the minutes of the last meeting being read and so on. After about a quarter hour, I felt a slight nudge at my elbow. I turned nonchalantly in her direction, and she whispered, "It's time to go."

"We can't go yet. People will think we just came for the free food."

"But that's exactly why we came," she returned.

"Let's give it a little more time," I urged. She nodded and a couple of minutes later she whispered again, "I have a plan. I brought my cane tonight, and with a little coughing and limping I'll make everyone think I'm an old woman, and you can escort me out to the back door." She was eighty-eight at the time. I couldn't believe what I was hearing, but I could see Aunt Kate and I think I saw pistols bulging from my mother's dress. The meeting dragged on, and I sensed it was going to be a long night. Her plan had some appeal. I thought it might be worth the gamble. The rebel was already on her feet.

"Now, remember, don't go too fast," she warned. She immediately produced a gentle cough, and a sad expression covered her face. Then a first step with a pronounced limp, and we were on our way. It took forever to round the first row of tables and head toward the back of the room, but my mother was enjoying every minute of it. She really looked old. With each step and a growing intensity to her cough, she aged a decade. Out of the corner of my eye, I saw sympathetic glances, and it was all I could do to keep a straight face. Another step, another cough, and we inched our way to the rear of the room where my ancient mother and I exited. When the door closed behind us, she straightened up, raised her cane, and burst out laughing. I joined in and, as I looked down at her, I remembered how often in my childhood on the farm she took a mundane situation and turned it into an extraordinary event, a wonderful memory. And she had done it again. We had escaped and left behind a room full of tear-streaked victims with a heartfelt compassion for a bona fide eighty-eight year old con artist.

Through the years, my mother and I morphed into a good team. Most of our regular dates occurred at the funeral home. She'd call and ask what I was doing on Thursday night, and I'd ask who died. I enjoyed taking her there, though, for the sole purpose of seeing friends' faces light up when they saw her. Somber countenances became happy ones as she moved among the crowd. People genuinely loved her. She greeted each with the same interest and dignity, looking eye to eye and asking some specific personal question concerning their family. I felt honored to be employed as Catherine the Great's bodyguard. However, the funeral home itself reminded me that someday she would be the guest of honor, and I would be unemployed.

Momma tried diligently to emulate her mother on the piano, but the natural talent wasn't there. I sensed her frustration. But when it came to memorizing and quoting poetry, she was a virtuoso. Her ability to recite with perfect timing and inflection was its own creative genius. She could quote epic poems effortlessly, making them reverberate with perfect pitch. Her mother played music, but Momma quoted music. One of my special treasures is a thirty-minute recording of her reciting her favorite poems. Sam Wich, a former student of mine, joined me one afternoon, unannounced, to film her recitations. She did not have time to look over or brush up on any of them. She just started speaking, and it flowed like a winding river of words. She was ninety years old.

Though she gave us her life, she did not reveal everything and kept a part of herself to herself, leaving us with a conundrum. On the surface, the title of her book, *Just Me*, indicated inferiority, but it was just another one of the games she played. *Just Me* was written tongue-in-cheek, with an air of mystery, a reminder of the rebel.

"Just me, funny? Oh, surely you don't mean me. Clever? Oh, not me. A rebel? You couldn't possibly be referring to me." What we thought of as a subservient housewife was only a disguise she used as she traveled across enemy lines, back and forth, day by day, the spy pretending to be the humble homemaker, but secretly raising a band of rebels.

Once, she was driving behind her daughters en route to a restaurant for supper. She grew impatient at their speed, so she passed them, arriving a few minutes ahead. When they pulled into the parking lot, they saw her slumped over the steering wheel. She had apparently passed out. The car door was locked, so they frantically banged on the window. After a few horror-stricken seconds, she slowly raised her head, revealed a huge smile, and laughed uncontrollably. The girls little appreciated the humor, but Momma explained that following them had almost bored her to death, so she had to move on.

At the age of ninety-two, my mother finally moved on, forever. No one was there. The nurses called us and we were trying our best to get there, but she wouldn't wait. She passed us. We were too slow. We bored her. She had somewhere to go, and this time she preferred no audience, no fanfare, and no bodyguard. Her prophetic book, *Just Me*, revealed who she wanted near when she left.

Of all the poems my mother knew, her favorite was William Cullen Bryant's *Thanatopsis*. It is a meditation upon death and concludes:

"So live, that when thy summons comes to join the innumerable caravan which moves to that mysterious realm, where each shall take his chamber in the silent halls of death, thou go not like the quarry slave at night scourged to his dungeon, but sustained and soothed by an unfaltering trust, approach thy grave like one who wraps the drapery of his couch about him and lies down to pleasant dreams."

The night before my mother's death, Ginny and I sat beside her bed, and the last act we performed for her was to wrap a blanket about her. Her countenance portrayed perfect trust, and that night she lay down to pleasant dreams. There she awaits us and, whatever heaven may be, it is a safe bet she feels at home there because heaven was created for rebels, and, of all those I have ever known or read about, Catherine the Great, my mother, was the quintessential rebel.

CHAPTER
FIVE

All the farm was a stage, and we were merely players. We had the same parents, but the similarities ceased there with my four siblings. As my father was fulfilling his dream of building a successful farm, my mother raised her children. Together they built a stage on which we, the players, rehearsed our parts, made our debuts, and performed. Props were constructed and scripts were rewritten daily. Some found themselves in the spotlight while others thrived as supporting actors. Some days we performed tragedies; other days were comedies, but the plot remained the same. We were a family, and we did our best with what we had in loving each other.

We ate my mother's home-cooked meals and discussed the farm around a green-stained circular table that sat in the middle of the kitchen. It was round, but no one questioned that it had a head. There existed a sense of freedom in expressing our opinions, as long as they did not stray too far from my father's. Each person sat in the same seat every day. From my perspective, my father sat at high noon. Moving clockwise was Teresa, the youngest; then my mother; I sat at 6:00, the antipodes. To my left was my brother, Chuck, then Linda, and finally Ginger, who anchored herself between Linda and my father.

We always began the meal with a prayer. Neither of our parents prayed at the table, so one of the children blessed the food, as we would say. I never understood the term "bless the food." Eggs are eggs, whether they are blessed or not. My digestive system never knew the difference. If I was asked to pray, I made a point to aim my prayer in the direction of my father. "Lord, help us not be so quick with our tongues. Lord, help us control our anger, Lord, help him, I mean us, not to…" I played the Pharisee, and prayer at the breakfast table was my only opportunity to have a voice. For some reason, the one praying had diplomatic immunity from the otherwise strict code of conduct we all lived under. The only advantage to my praying was that it took valuable time away from the expected argument each morning. When I finished, everyone was hungry, and a full mouth is counterproductive to verbal disagreements.

Every family has its own vocabulary. Irreverent words that included swearing or the taking of God's name in vain were forbidden. On the second tier were the four letter words we grew up with but were unsure of their origins and why they were bad. I once said the word *damn* to myself just to hear it. I was not impressed. If pumpernickel or flabbergast had been juicy curse words, I'd be a buccaneer today; cussing would have been dignified. But four-letter words are syllable challenged, offering no real edification for the intellect. My father's vocabulary had grown substantially, we were told, in the Navy, and he shared those words with us occasionally, complete with emphasis. I did not have to be taught that the root word in discussion was cuss. There were few words that were taboo in our family, but there were two that held reverential status.

The only occasion in which we were allowed to use the word pregnant was in reference to animals. Cows were pregnant; sows were pregnant; horses, cats, and dogs were pregnant, but women were … well, no one ever said. We openly talked about a cow's vagina or uterus. We discussed the swollen vulva of a cow in heat and what that meant. My father taught me that a healthy uterine discharge resembled the clear white of an egg before it is cooked, and an unhealthy discharge the opaque color of the egg white after cooking. In severe infections, the discharge was full of pus and resembled the gravy made from flour and minute steak. So we discussed these things over breakfast, while eating the opaque-colored fried eggs and creamy brown gravy that spilled over the biscuits. It seemed perfectly normal, but we never talked about a pregnant woman.

The other word was divorce. To my mother any four-letter word was better than this one. I only heard the word spoken once, when my father was in a Navy mood. It stopped my mother cold. She didn't balk at words like murder, decapitation, or other words found in horror books. As a matter of fact, she once bought me a book about the history of the violence of the Chicago mob, complete with grotesque, graphic pictures of bloody dead men. Actually, it was a whole series of books that made up a complete set in ten volumes. It gave me nightmares, and I had to stop reading them. But these were macabre events, not divorce.

To my mother, there were lines that could not be crossed. To kill a spouse had its merits, but to divorce was completely out of the question. It was the eleventh commandment, and God held a special place in His Inferno for such people. I did not grow up with a healthy respect for marriage, nor did I consider it a happy institution, but it was impressed upon me from the beginning that once a promise was made to another person in the presence of God and other witnesses, nothing came between them. There was no turning back. My mother's commitment on marriage dwarfed Julius Caesar's crossing of the Rubicon. When one said, "I do," the die was cast.

Words are powerful. Family conversations around our kitchen table were often little more than outward manifestations of strong personalities. Like a pinball machine, the conversations were unpredictable. We never knew where the ball would bounce, setting off whistles and lights, scoring big points, or losing everything in the blink of an eye. Just when the game seemed destined to end, someone would utter another opinion, and it started all over again. No one had a better knack at keeping this wrecking ball swinging than my eldest sister, Linda.

Linda was nine years older than I was, and still is, but nine years was different when I was seven. She appeared grown up, not like my mother, but more like an aunt who never forgot my birthday. Her lanky, athletic frame exhibited a feminine strength, and she appeared all legs to me. Her soft face resembled Aunt Helen's, but her blonde hair and determined blue eyes gave her a distinctly Viking look. She was funny and light-hearted in her approach to life, while maintaining her safe distance relationally. She was the firstborn and carried a burden the rest of us little understood.

She did her best to encourage us. Once, I walked up behind her as she worked on a sewing project. I peered over her shoulder and saw a stuffed monkey being sewn together. "What are you making?" I asked. Without flinching or hesitation, as if she had rehearsed for days, she replied, "I'm making a doll for a little boy who doesn't have one." She returned to her work, and I walked away to my room in pity for that poor child. A month later at Christmas I unwrapped the monkey. She was like that, and I loved her.

Her relationship with our father was always troubled, but she never wavered. She was who she was, and no one was going to change her. Always the actress, except with him, Linda was going to be loved for who she was or not at all. The stage disappeared, and the mask came off. We silently begged for the actress, but she would have none of it. Each morning we congregated at the kitchen table for breakfast. Being on time was imperative to my father. No one started eating until all were present. The curtain went up each morning. When in a good mood, Linda floated across the floor, did a pirouette, and slid into her seat like a wisp of perfume. We inhaled deeply, taking in the aroma while exhaling with relief the avoidance of another tragic dialogue between her and our father. But on a bad day, it was all "double, double toil and trouble," and the cauldron bubbled over as she entered the kitchen on the wings of disaster. Like a kamikaze pilot, she knew what lay in store, but her stubborn unwillingness to yield kept her dedicated to the cause. And though we did not share the cockpit, we were passengers, and when she crashed, we perished with her.

Before I had time to really focus on her, Linda went away to college where she quickly married and seldom returned. I missed her. She left an indelible mark on me that I barely recognized until much later. It would be fair, however, to say I didn't miss the intense dialogues at the table each morning. I anticipated a season of peace. I was ignorant, however, that her early retirement only left a vacancy to be filled. The show had to go on, and Chuck, without knowing it, was next in line. Without his approval, he appeared front stage under a spotlight for which he was ill prepared.

Chuck was three years younger than Linda, and he resembled my mother's side of the family. Quiet and introspective, he reminded my mother of her grandfather who worked with his hands as a builder. For Chuck everything was patience and precision—just the attributes that brought him into direct conflict with my father who saw a job as a project, not a piece of artwork. When one is given the name of his father, there is an unwritten expectation that their aspirations and dreams will coincide and, when they don't, some fathers find it impossible to accept those differences. My father wanted Chuck to be someone different. It wasn't clear what, but it was clear that simply being Chuck wasn't enough.

I remember the morning my father threw a Mason jar at him across the kitchen table (where most epic battles took place). Chuck was standing near the door leading into the dining room.

57

It shattered about a foot above his head. Chuck never flinched. No words were exchanged. They both left the room, heading in opposite directions. I knew he had not meant to hit him. Daddy could throw a baseball a hundred feet and hit a Coke bottle every time. My brother knew this as well, and probably regarded the near miss to his head as a type of affection. I followed Chuck outside, and as we got into the Dodge truck to haul sawdust, he looked over at me and said, "I think it's time for me to leave home. If I stay much longer, we won't have any glasses left to drink out of."

When I was eight years old, or thereabouts, I found myself in a precarious situation one afternoon behind the small shed where we raised baby calves. Gene Miller, whose father worked for us, confronted me. I didn't see him coming, and when I turned around, he stood ominous, like the Colossus of Rhodes. We were the same age, and I was a hair taller, but his rough upbringing hardened him into a monumental force, and I was terrified of him.

Gene, I was told, had smoked cigars since birth. He started chewing tobacco when he was 5, and I stared at him that day in mortal fear. His jaw was packed with a huge chaw of tobacco. He rolled it around, puckered his lips and spit at my feet.

"I'm gonna whup ya," he seethed, and he used his barefoot to toe a line in the dirt between us.

He didn't give a reason, which I thought would have been, at least, respectful, but his awareness of such social norms obviously lay hidden. In his home, beatings were common, so I started slowly to retreat when I heard my brother's voice some distance away, behind me, across a fence.

"Don't budge, Gilbert, show him who is boss. He's only a Miller."

His being a Miller didn't seem to be relevant at that moment, except that being a Miller meant he was meaner and tougher than I was. He spat again at my feet.

"Ya gonna run, chicken?"

When he compared me to a chicken, a great hope surged in me because chickens were fast. But my brother continued to draw a line behind me with his admonitions that indicated only a coward would run.

Gene inched forward and spat again, this time hitting my boot.

"Let's play a game, chicken," his voice swaggered. "I'll say a word, and you say it backwards."

I thought he only knew how to smoke, dip, and fight. I never considered he could spell. I was stunned, but I kept silent. He began.

"Or."

"Ro," I mechanically stammered.

"But"

"Tub," It was getting easier.

It was all a setup, because the next came in the form of two words.

"Mad dog"

What came out of my mouth must have rattled the gates of hell. The sound stunned me, and without thinking, my fist hardened into a ball, and I swung wildly and found my target, his eye. Gene hit the ground. His look of amazement surprised me. He jumped up and took off toward home. It was then that I heard Chuck laughing and praising me.

"I'm proud of you, brother."

He didn't often call me brother, so it was mesmerizing. I never turned around to see him. The words were enough. I straightened up, arranged my britches as if I were adjusting my six-shooter, then I sauntered away into the sunset. Drawing the line behind me, my brother taught me to set my feet firmly when confronted, not to retreat. To this day when fear grips me, I hear his words, "Don't budge, Gilbert; I'm proud of you, brother."

But Chuck was seldom content. He went from mini bike to motorcycle to Harley-Davidson—always bigger and faster. He stayed out late at night riding, and Daddy made him work that much harder the next day, but Chuck never complained. He had fortitude and a resolve short of miraculous. But years of this personality war affected Chuck. Internally, he was always compassionate and kind, but Chuck was porous, and eventually my father began to seep in and erode his nature. Boys are born with a reservoir only a father's love and acceptance can fill. If not filled, a boy will seek to fill it in other ways. A boy needs a hero, and if he cannot have one, he will be his own. Like many boys, Chuck sought to be his own in the military at the height of the Vietnam War.

Chuck enrolled at Middle Tennessee State University. He wanted to join the Army, but my father forbade it. At freshman orientation, though, Chuck was the only student who refused the draft board notification as a student. This increased his chances of being drafted. He was certified 1A, putting him in the top spot for selection in the televised draft.

We finished eating supper and gathered in the den in front of the television. Momma joined us after doing the dishes. The rules were explained. A birth date was read out and then a number, from 1 to 365, for each day of the year was chosen corresponding to the birth date. The larger the number, the less likely one went to Vietnam. This was Chuck's night. This time the U.S. Government would have the final say, and my father could do nothing about it. Chuck told me he wanted to prove himself, and Vietnam represented his best opportunity. We listened to date after date, when finally August twenty-fifth came up. It seemed an eternity until the linked number was read: 364. We all cheered, except Chuck. He quietly rose and left the room.

If Chuck had been deployed to Vietnam, he would have either been killed, become a hero, or both. His sense of loyalty and his reckless courage would have kept him near a fallen comrade. To Chuck there was no middle ground. Abandonment was not part of his agenda. This is not mere speculation, because years later, when his only son drowned in Dry Fork and his bereaved wife suffered a nervous breakdown, Chuck somehow held both her and himself together. Later, when she was bedridden and dying of emphysema, he never flinched in his devotion. He stayed by her side and nurtured her on a different sort of battlefield. When I was very young, I idolized my brother simply because he was my older brother. As I grew up, I placed him on a more substantial pedestal based on his unwavering commitment to those he loved.

Ginger represented the fulcrum in the sibling lineup: the proverbial middle child. Her goal in life was to be a peacekeeper. She would have been a peacemaker, but that takes a lot of time and energy. In our family, success was measured in the short run. If, at the end of the day, no Mason jars had flown, all was right with the world and Ginger, more than any of us, had the ability to pull it off. Where many of Linda's antics loom boldly in my memory like a bright summer's day, Ginger's quiet acts of love and service linger like a misty morning. She often went unnoticed, as supporting cast members do, but when her cue came, her words and actions were always encouraging. She didn't know how to be judgmental; that is the beauty of a fulcrum. It provides balance for all at its own expense. It allows others to go up and down with the moodiness of their own selfishness while it gently, patiently waits for the return to normalcy.

Ginger attended Bellwood School, and was in the fourth grade when I was in the first grade. I cried every day and asked to see her. They allowed me to go to her room, where she sat with me until I gained enough confidence to return to my room. She was my mother–sister that year. In college, I always sought out her advice on a variety of issues. I had just begun dating Ginny, and we wrote many letters to each other. When I got one, I immediately took it to Ginger. I sat anxiously while she read it and gave me her interpretation. She encouraged and kept me confident that someone out there might actually find me interesting.

Ginger played high school basketball for a coach who seldom gave her the opportunity. She never had Linda's confidence, but Ginger was tenacious on the court. One of my greatest regrets was the night Ginger played her final high school game. I stayed home to watch a documentary on the OK Corral. Even today, the mention of that historical event brings a degree of sadness, not because of the men who died there but because I let my sister down, the one who nurtured me so often. I did, however, get my revenge on her coach several years later when he coached at a nearby county school. He had good teams, and when he brought his heavily favored boys to Webb, all I could think about was Ginger. We completely destroyed them that night. We gunned them down like Wyatt Earp and Doc Holliday did at the OK Corral a hundred years before. That one was for Ginger.

I was the fourth child and, for reasons unknown, I always felt left out. My father favored me primarily because we had similar interests. This favoritism made me feel distant from my siblings. One morning at the kitchen table he said he wished the rest of them were like me. He didn't really mean it, but I hated it. Actually, I wanted to be more like them. They had to put on their masks at times to play their parts, but they were always able to take them off. I could not tell when mine was off or on.

As a high school freshman, I read Hawthorne's *The Great Stone Face* during a study hall. I finished it, shut the book, and cried to myself right there in the middle of the library. I wanted to be that face, since I didn't have one of my own. It was so noble, so worth spending a lifetime pursuing. Now, years later, the face I yearned for has weathered under the erosion of my own shortcomings. It seems more important to me now to wear my face simply because it is uniquely mine, chiseled by daily living. It is not great, and no one in the valley is watching, but it is, nonetheless, part of humanity's landscape.

So I grew up pleasing others. Happy the man who has no reputation to protect. I seldom found myself in the spotlight and, consequently, seldom found myself in conflict. Besides, it was more interesting as a spectator of the family drama. The difficulty with being a spectator, however, is that one is never a part of the drama, and I think that was the hardest part of growing up. But no matter how lonely or difficult life was, I always had Teresa, my younger sister by eighteen months.

I once asked Momma if Teresa was a surprise. Without hesitation, she said we were all surprises. She left it at that and walked away. Teresa and I did everything together, especially when it came to observing our siblings act out their parts. We discussed the play as the drama unfolded. We learned so much from the others. We read the expressions in each face as conversations developed, and we looked at each other and remarked, "That was not the best way to handle that," "His body language just created a bomb," or "That was good, I'll try that one later." I consider being born at the end of the lineup a blessing. It did not help me become me, but it taught me how to survive.

Teresa had an unusual way of expressing affection to me in the form of her pointed middle finger curled in a protruding knuckle, which she drove into my sternum with great force. It hurt, but the feeling of love and goodwill from which it originated compensated for the pain. To my knowledge, no one else ever received this special brand of love. Most of our time together was spent working, so we found the humor in the everyday. Once, I was walking behind a cow as she left the milking parlor. I was trying to be cute by mimicking Teresa, and I had my mouth open. The cow coughed and filled my mouth with manure. My eyes and throat burned, and my nose went into convulsions, but I could hear Teresa laughing in the background. I loved her voice, and I again felt the protruding knuckle.

From early on, Teresa was extremely attractive. None of us were aware that other boys lived on our road until she reached her teenage years, and a small migration of young bucks made their way to our habitat. These finely arrayed boys came from far and wide to play basketball on Saturday afternoons. For years, I thought they enjoyed playing with me, but I learned later I was only the excuse to get closer to her. My mother, well aware of Teresa's good looks, often said, "Pity the pretty girl." I hardly understood the maxim because Teresa had so many friends, and I had so few. I thought pity might more appropriately be allocated to the ugly. Anyway, Momma wanted to keep her protected from the world, so there were restrictions placed on her wardrobe: the more wardrobe, the better. One hot, July day Teresa was cutting the grass in her halter top and skimpy cutoff shorts. Momma called her in and said there was too much skin. Teresa went to her room, and the next time we saw her she had returned to the push-mower in rubber boots, long blue jeans, a wool long-sleeve shirt, a scarf, ski mask, and sock hat. She cut the remainder of that huge yard in the extreme heat. Momma laughed so hard she cried. I think she was proud of the rebel. Aunt Kate lived on.

In my teenage years, summer was the most wonderful season because our family spent long days together. At four-thirty each morning, we milked the cows and fed the calves. Momma always had eggs and biscuits for breakfast, then we went back out to do a varied list of jobs. Teresa and I played chess at lunchtime, and the game went on for weeks as we made only a move or two before going back out. We milked twice a day, every day, and the conversations with my sisters during those couple of hours were often philosophical and humorous. As I came of age on Gordon's Villa, the adage, "Sisters are the perfect best friend" could not have been more true. It was the best of times.

But they all grew up, left home, and the farm turned quiet and introspective. The time went by so quickly and that life was never the same again. My daughter, Hannah, recently told me that "You can't be what you are today without having been what you were then." I like that. With the passing of my father and mother, the curtain finally came down on that stage, but the rest of us are still connected to those few years on Rock Springs Road where we acted out our parts the best we knew and loved each other with a purity found only among siblings. The strong bonds we treasure today were forged by the way we were then.

CHAPTER
SIX

As close as we may have been as a family, there were times when each of us needed a place to find ourselves and take a respite from the others. Linda found her place at our grandparents, where she was loved just for being Linda. Chuck mounted a Harley and found peace in the open air. Ginger did not have to leave home, but found her place when she helped others find theirs, and Teresa found peace on the bareback of a horse somewhere on the farm. My place was on Mrs. Eunice Holden's front porch. She was our nearest neighbor, and lived directly across the road from us with her husband. His health had been failing for years due to what we called palsy, a constant shaking of the body. When he died, apart from being alone, her life changed little. She spent most of her day in the front porch swing, and as often as I could, I joined her in the evenings to enjoy her stories.

Beauty settles in the eyes, and hers were deep-caverns and distinct. The dark circles that on others reflect anxiety and fatigue adorned her as rouge on a blushing bride. Her eyes revealed a woman of contentment, gained not by a life of ease but through hardship. With a long, angular face supporting a sharp, protruding chin, Mrs. Eunice possessed a country-type of elegance. She was thin all over, not an emaciated thin but a refined thin that must have turned the eyes of many men in her day. Even her voice was razor sharp, concise and to the point. I can't remember her wearing anything other than the same pale blue full-length dress that could have been cut up and made into nice, thin dusting cloths. It hung on her like the branches of a cedar tree after a snow, and I often wondered if she ever took it off. She was what a grandmother should look like, and I thought she was beautiful.

Exuding a demeanor of acceptance, she absorbed me and made me feel her life was made richer by my short visits. Crossing the road to her home was entering another world, going back in time, and a place where I rested from the anxieties of our farm. I heard stories about her childhood that I hardly remember now, but the telling of them was intoxicating. She took me to the past, and on that that small porch allowed me passage into her world, a passage few had the privilege of entering, or at least she made me feel that way. Her recent memorable story involved her grandson. She told him she had fallen because she lost her balance. To this he responded, "Well, let's find you another one." Every time she told this story, her head cocked back, thrusting her nose high into the air, and she laughed like it had just happened. Memory is a great gift, and Mrs. Eunice unwrapped hers daily.

On days when the weather wasn't pleasant enough to sit on the porch, or if we just needed a change of atmosphere, she invited me inside for her homemade sugar cookies. The recipe was simple: flour, sugar, and eggs. I couldn't wait to have a few. She kept them in a round tin that was never empty. Sometimes we watched TV together, but eventually story time came, and we moved to the parlor. The interior of her home contrasted with the bland exterior that her husband had assembled. Decorated with dainty doilies and fringes, her parlor's elegance enticed me to take off my shoes before entering. It was the kind of room roped off from the tourists in historic homes. Each wall held pictures of her family, and she was so proud of her children and grandchildren. These were the ones who filled most of her stories.

Her front yard was nondescript, except for the large catalpa tree near the road. Each summer when the catalpa worms emerged to strip it of its leaves, I filled up a tin can with them and went fishing for channel catfish. An empty, open-fronted carless garage sat at the end of a grassy driveway. Behind her house was a very small building resembling a bunkhouse, which she told me had been their one-room home for most of their married life. Behind this, a narrow path led to an outhouse that she still used into her eighties. It was a simple landscape, like Mrs. Eunice.

I cut her grass and, though I tried not to take payment, she insisted on two dollars. She had a small blue handbag where she kept her money. She gingerly opened it and carefully pulled out the two dollars, one at a time. It gave her a degree of satisfaction. With the two dollars came a warm smile. She looked at me with those penetrating eyes and said, "Thank you for a job well done." The words were more valuable than the money, but being a Gordon I knew I couldn't deposit words, so I collected and stuffed them in the pocket of my blue jeans.

One summer she hired me to cut and weed her family cemetery. Dead family members were no less important to her than the living ones. So each week I loaded my push lawnmower into the bed of our old Ford 150, drove about a mile down the asphalt road, turned onto a dead-end gravel drive, and parked near the cemetery's entrance gate. It was flanked on either side by two huge, rough-cut stone pillars, each about two feet square and six feet tall. They were massive and gave the cemetery more prominence than necessary. Rusty web-wire fence encircled the remainder of the graveyard, which included groundhog holes, old maple trees, and leftover plastic flowers from previous burials. Mrs. Eunice paid me by the week, which meant during rainy weather I worked much harder to keep it manicured than during droughts. This discrepancy led me to consider an alternative—a better mousetrap.

Brilliant ideas fill my portfolio. Once, I took a flower wreath and its stand from a recent burial, replaced the dead flowers with pretty weeds and gave it to my mother on her fiftieth birthday. She smiled, but I could see her envisioning a four-by eight-foot hole in the ground. Or the time I heard the price of stamps was going up, so I went to the post office to order several rolls at the current price. Or the time I rode a stallion down to a group of mares to get one of them bred. Thought I'd just stay on him while he did his business, and ride him back to the barn. I wasn't married at the time, and gave little thought to how inconvenient it might be for the stallion. When he bucked, I hit the ground on my back, knocking the air out of me. I surmised he knew best about his love life.

But the idea concerning lawn mowing was different, and it came in the form of a billy goat. A goat resembles the modern automatic lawnmower that moves itself about the lawn, crisscrossing in perfect patterns to ensure complete coverage in a twenty-four hour period. Such machines require batteries and occasionally malfunction. Goats, however, without the aid of algorithms, do the same job, require no batteries, and their by-product fertilizes the grass. It was the perfect solution to my hands-off enterprise.

My billy goat was sleek and jet black, with a prominent beard and pointed ears, giving him the appearance of a goblin on Halloween. I named him Satan. He reared up on his hind legs at my approach and put his hooves on the wire fence and we stood eye to eye. He terrorized my sisters as they passed through the lot leading to the barn. For some reason he hated females, so everyone rejoiced when I announced I would be moving him to his new home in the Holden cemetery.

We rode together to the graveyard where I unloaded him, gave him a pan of water, and christened him my newfound financial security. Every Saturday afternoon I visited Satan. He ran up to the fence, reared up on his hind legs, and I stroked his beard, though it always smelled like urine (goats have a few undesirable habits). After our ritual, I took my small broom and dusted off all of his biodegradables from each flat gravestone. I couldn't help admiring how nice everything looked and how little work I had expended. With the job completed, I said goodbye and returned home.

I received a call late one evening from Mrs. Eunice. Her voice spoke of tragedy. She said her aunt had visited the cemetery that evening. I don't remember how old the aunt was, but Mrs. Eunice was in her upper eighties. Apparently, the aunt arrived at dusk with her nephew who stayed in the car, giving her the opportunity for time alone with her relatives. She approached the front gate nostalgically and peered over to get a panoramic view. Satan reared up before her in all his charm, glory, and odor. Their eyes met in the twilight. I can only imagine their conversation. Mrs. Eunice spared me the details, but she kindly asked if I would extradite the apparition back across the farm line. Then her voice grew quiet, and I thought I heard a faint snicker, but only momentarily. Composure regained, she said good night, and I retrieved Satan immediately that evening.

A week later, I returned to the cemetery to witness the burial of the traumatized aunt. Meeting Satan must have been too much for her. She entered through the stone pillars horizontally. There were only a few of us there, including Mrs. Eunice who wore a peculiar grin, something between laughter and reverence. The eulogy was short, and as we exited back through the gate, Mrs. Eunice stopped, turned, and viewed the graveyard as if inspecting it. Then she turned to me and commented on how nice everything looked, followed by a wink meant only for me.

I continued to spend many evenings on her porch, listening to the stories, snacking on sugar cookies, laughing about things that weren't funny, and relaxing. Sometimes in mid-sentence she'd stop and look out across the road toward our house, then she refocused and the story went on. She listened to me when I tried to tell a story, and she laughed as if I were the greatest storyteller telling the greatest story. Many times, I didn't even finish my tale when she'd exclaim how good it was, and the prominent chin would rise in glee. I discovered later that she was almost deaf by this time.

Returning from her home one afternoon, my father stopped me as I crossed the road. He asked me why I spent so much time with Mrs. Eunice. I thought it was an odd question. *Why does anyone spend time with another person? Why do we seek out the company and conversation of people with whom we feel at ease?* Before I could speak, he revealed the answer: "You must love her more than your grandmother" (his mother). His inflection stung, and he gazed at me to insure that all of the poison was injected before allowing me to walk away and privately pull out the stinger.

My father's acts of kindness toward many were legion, but his words could negate a lifetime of service. He loved Mrs. Eunice and showed it by caring for her land and making repairs on her house. He was even instrumental in getting her an indoor toilet. So I never understood the point of his comment. I did know, however, that it cut me to the quick and altered my visits to her front porch. Many evenings I saw her sitting, peering across the road, waiting for me, but I could not remove the guilt he had so effectively planted. To spend time with her was to reject my grandmother. It was a lose–lose–lose situation. I think my father sensed her loneliness, but he wasn't in the habit of apologizing. I still cut her yard, and I loved her, but it wasn't the same. Soon afterward, I moved away to college and visited her in letters.

My grandmother died the year before I married, so I asked Mrs. Eunice to stand in for her at our wedding. She agreed enthusiastically. On the day of the wedding, she was wheeled down the aisle in a beautiful green dress, purchased just for the occasion. It was no more impressive than her blue one to me. Regardless of her attire, I was just glad she was there.

A month later, after our honeymoon, we returned home for a few days and visited her. I boldly crossed the road with my new bride and walked up the steps where she was rocking in the porch swing with the old cookie tin on a nearby table. She had heard we were home. I felt ashamed that I had neglected her in those few years, but here she was today, and we took our seats near her. The years weighed heavily upon her, but she smiled and was about to tell us something when she stopped and looked across the yard as she did so many times. Then she turned and those dark eyes peered out whimsically. "Guess what my grandson said just the other day when I lost my balance?" I grabbed a sugar cookie, sat back, and listened to a country saint unwrap another memory in story. I was home again.

CHAPTER
SEVEN

The distance between homesteads is no indication of the quality
of relationships in the rural community. Because our existence is
based on the soil we live on, it is ultimately the land that connects
us. And so, neighbors on Rock Springs Road are people whose
lands meet, even if miles separate their homes. This was the case
with the Mitchells. The Gordon and Mitchell farms covered more
than three of the four miles on our road, and we spent a lot of time
helping each other. Farmers are peculiar. They are willing to go the
extra mile to help a neighbor, but there is a delicate balance keeping
anyone from beholding too much to anyone else. There is respect

mingled with pride, allowing each family a way to maintain its autonomy without appearing reclusive.

Uncle Dan and Miss Barbara Mitchell were our neighbors; they were married. He wasn't really our uncle, but should have been. He didn't receive the title of uncle by accomplishing some noble deed. There was no official ceremony, no ringing of the bells. He just seemed like an uncle through his daily love and acceptance of our family, and so he was our Uncle Dan.

He always wore overalls, which kept us from knowing exactly how he was put together physically. Just short of tall, rounding but solid, he owned a smile that erupted into a full-blown grin at the drop of a hat. He never enjoyed the warmth of a full head of hair, giving him an aura of wisdom. Although he strove to make his own farm successful, he always took time to help his neighbors. He never had urgency to his stride, and would have made an upright judge.

Miss Barbara didn't possess the title of aunt, but she was every bit the complement of her husband. Her gentleness and grace moved softly with her wherever she went. We called her Miss Barbara, and she appeared more like Uncle Dan's daughter than his wife, explaining why the aunt designation just didn't work. I once saw a picture hanging on the wall near their stairway and was struck by the extraordinary beauty of the girl. The Mitchell home was not typically decorated with any degree of worldliness, and this photograph of a Hollywood starlet seemed out of place. I squinted, examined it closely, and finally asked, "Who is this beautiful woman?" Miss Barbara stared at me incredulously. Then slowly a smile appeared. A telling twinkle emerged from her countenance, and I immediately recognized her in the picture. I marveled that Uncle Dan had snared such a prize. I have noticed that men of dubious attractiveness often lure the finest catches. Women are deeper than men, and aren't overly impressed with the package. They love unconditionally. Miss Barbara was such a woman.

My earliest memories of her were Sunday afternoons in the summer when I went home with their sons, David and Joe, after church. She took us to the creek and patiently waited as we waded around the mossy water. We caught crawfish and pretended to be heroes and villains. She was never in a hurry and enjoyed our fun as if it were her own. At times her youthfulness pulled her into the water, and she splashed along with us as a child would. She was ageless.

Uncle Dan lived in the same house where he was born. His father died when he was only twelve years old, leaving him head of the family, His mother, Mrs. Carrie, was a no-nonsense woman who had lived through the Depression, twice it seemed. She had a low center of gravity. Her gray hair was always wound up in a knot on top of her head, which would have been more beautiful if I had not perceived it as a reflection of her tightly screwed personality. She walked as if always headed for an appointment, head down, thinking, her expression serious, if not austere. Life had taught her survival. The death of her husband was preceded by the deaths of two infants. Unaccustomed to real tragedy at ten years of age, I thoughtlessly asked her once if she ever got over the pain of losing her children. Pouring lemonade at a vacation bible school picnic, she stopped and took a long look at me, searching for the right words, then replied drearily, "I'll let you know when I do." She resumed pouring the lemonade and said nothing more. She was well into her seventies then.

When Uncle Dan and Miss Barbara married, they moved into his mother's home. Much has been said about two cooks in the same kitchen, mostly in the way of harmless jokes, but there was nothing funny or healthy about those two women in that house. Too young to really understand the dynamics of this cohabitation, I still at times picked up on the strain. Mrs. Carrie considered her daughter-in-law an intruder, and I wondered if there wasn't a bit of jealousy for taking away the only son she had. But in spite of this arrangement, Miss Barbara and Uncle Dan exuded a beautiful marriage, and their love for one another was evident. Mrs. Carrie was doing her best to tread life, but as a drowning person will do in the struggle, she pulled desperately at those closest to her.

One afternoon while working under the shade tree in front of our milk barn, I noticed in the distance a strange figure weaving aimlessly across our cornfield. It reminded me of a rabid dog taking a few steps, stopping, looking around, and then ambling off in another direction. But this was a man, and he eventually made his way to the barn. It was Uncle Dan. My father met him at the gate, and I could tell something was terribly wrong. He leaned on Daddy as they both inched their way to the steps of the milk barn. There, he slumped down onto the concrete, put his head in his hands and began to sob. The man who always wore a smile was crying. I made out only a little bit, but he was saying he couldn't make them both happy anymore. His attempt at balancing his devotion to his mother and his great love for his wife brought him to an impasse. Although the wedding vows stressed that one should leave his parents and cleave to his spouse, he allowed economics and compassion to bypass sound wisdom, and it created an unbearable tension.

There were, however, happy moments in living near the Mitchells. One Saturday morning when Daddy and Uncle Dan were talking together in our front driveway, our German shepherd meandered up, hiked his leg, and saturated Uncle Dan's pant leg. Both men stared unflinchingly at the dog in amazement until he had completely finished. Then, simultaneously, they looked up at each other. Without expression or hesitation, my father said, "Dan, around here you have to keep moving or the dogs think you are a tree." They both exploded in laughter.

Uncle Dan was a storyteller, and he was privileged to be born in the midst of a vast array of colorful personalities, namely my family. He wrote a book entitled, *Gordon Men I Have Known*, in which he told their stories. Some of the tales, however, were too colorful for print, so from time to time he pulled me aside and gave me the R-rated version. But every time he got to the R-rated part, he broke out in laughter, and it took him forever to finish. Sometimes he just walked away shaking his head, talking to himself.

I don't remember meeting Uncle Dan and Miss Barbara. Like the old maple tree that stood in our front yard, they went unnoticed as we lived out our lives together. One night the old maple fell, and the next day I noticed what was missing due to its absence. I noticed the shade that was no longer available, the absence of birds singing in its branches, and the missing shadow, indicating the time of day.

The Mitchells were that way, and with the illness and eventual passing of Uncle Dan I noticed the absence of a number of things: the stroll down Rock Springs Road of a couple still in love, the voice of one who told me stories of my family and our disappearing community, the lessons in politics, the wisdom of raising children, and the impersonations of the Gordon men he knew so well. He provided shade and a song throughout my life, but it was natural, like the maple tree, not something to notice or say thank you for, just something to bask in while it was available. But when he also fell, I realized, in part, what a great treasure I had lost.

In the last few days of his life, preparations for moving him to a nursing home were made, but the great storyteller had the final word and died in the east room thirty feet from the bed on which he was born. Seventy-nine years of living in the same home, going to the same barn, loving his wife, respecting his mother, raising two boys, and influencing five generations of the Gordon family. You can't forget a man like Uncle Dan. He gets under your skin. His voice and expressions are indelible, and he did what all great men do. He cast a perpetual shadow on my life, and it is in the shade and comfort of that shadow I continue to live.

After his death, Miss Barbara stayed a couple of years at the old home place. She came to our house on many evenings to watch a movie or just to talk about him. We looked at stacks of old pictures and reminisced, and laughed and cried. She particularly enjoyed watching the old westerns with the upright heroes. They reminded her of him. She never tired of talking about her boys and how proud she was of them. She was also thankful for her daughters-in-law, the daughters she never had. She seemed to heal a bit with each visit.

She was not an avid gardener, but for a year or two each spring she planted one faithfully with the same vegetables he would have planted as a tribute to her gardening husband. She said it was easier seeing him there if the familiar plants grew in his well-established rows. Some widows wear black, she planted a garden. Eventually the mourning period had its effect, and she was able to let go of the soil, first, and then her home. She moved to town and started a new life with new friends at the Stones River Home for Beautiful People. Her grandson and his family moved into her home to begin their lives together as a newly married couple. Miss Barbara left them to themselves without interference, a privilege that was denied her.

Then she died on Christmas Eve the next year. Suddenly, without notice, she died. She had come to our house the previous night, and we had another great time laughing about what we always laughed about, and the next day she was gone. Uncle Dan had passed away. Gradually he left us, giving us time to say goodbye and prepare. Passing away is watching the sun slowly set. The reality of the coming night is offset by the beautiful hues of the sunset. But Miss Barbara's departure was ecliptic. It was sunny, then it was not. No sunset, just the sudden chill of a cold and lonely darkness.

Miss Barbara took up residence in the Gordon Cemetery on Rock Springs Road in the community where she and her husband had lived together for so long. Several years before, we had all tried to persuade Uncle Dan to make his final resting place in this community. Although his heart was in the country, his promise to his mother to be buried beside her in the city trumped our attempts. But what he could not do for himself, his sons did for him. Shortly after Miss Barbara was buried, Uncle Dan was exhumed, hauled on a flat-bed trailer, and reburied beside his wife in a quiet section of their new home in the country beneath the cedar trees overlooking the community they knew and loved so well.

People sanctify a place. Our neighbors brought reverence to our lives, not because they were perfect but because they were always there. They saw us at our best and worst, but stayed with us, and we, in turn, did the same. We have rejoiced together at births in hospitals, raised glasses in toasts at weddings in churches, and mourned together in cemeteries. A special bond exists between old dance partners. Even if we get out of step at times and step on each other's toes, when the music fades away, there remains a sense of devotion and love in a community that only time has the power to create.

CHAPTER
EIGHT

Parents devise a multitude of schemes to coax their children into staying in their beds at night. The most effective means is, of course, fear. "There's a monster under the bed." In medieval times, children were threatened with having their blood sucked out by vampires. When I was six years old and heard the tale of Jim Mallard for the first time, the thought of a large bat would have been less frightening than this man. The horrific possibility of his returning to my bedroom at night struck a fear that kept me tucked in under my quilts deep into the night.

Jim Mallard watched the glow of the burning corncribs illuminate the night sky. He set them ablaze to get his Uncle Sam and Aunt Nancy out of their log house in order to rob them. The elderly brother and sister exited on cue and made their way across the road to the corncribs to put out the fire. Jim then slipped into their home. He found what he thought he was looking for—their life's savings of four hundred dollars. But as he turned to leave, he noticed an official-looking yellow-stained document pressed between two envelopes. It was their will. In disbelief he read that they were dividing their entire estate, about $29,000, between all the members of the family, except him. With this revelation, Jim immediately set in motion a series of inconceivable events that led to the Gordon family acquiring the farm on which I grew up.

The 1920s were an eclectic time in American history. For the top three percent of the population, who controlled one third of the wealth, it was an age of optimism. President Calvin Coolidge promoted business as a panacea. Industrial wages increased, but not as fast as corporate earnings, and the gap between the rich and the poor grew. At the same time, farm income dove to new lows coming off of the WWI boom. Millions of acres were abandoned, and those who farmed found alternative means of living. Matters were especially desperate on farms with marginal land, like that which existed on Rock Springs Road.

With financial struggles came the temptation of illicit employment. With Prohibition, the perfect storm arose and created men like Al Capone in Chicago and a softening of justice from the general population who needed the alcohol to dull the everyday reality of poverty. To draw a parallel between Al Capone and Jim Mallard and the times in which they lived might be a bit of a stretch, but it might shed some light on the extraordinary events and the responses to those events concerning this story.

These factors contributed to the atmosphere that some say produced Jim Mallard. It is difficult to analyze him except through sketchy comments passed down from generation to generation. It was true that there were desperate farmers in poverty, but it was equally true that some farmers prospered in spite of the conditions. It was true that a blind eye toward crime prevailed during these years in this area as the residents concentrated more on survival than justice. But it was also true that law and order still held the day. Character and integrity are independent of social conditions, and when life applies pressure, truth comes out much like water from a sponge. What oozed out of Jim was dark and deadly.

Much speculation has risen over the years as to Jim's mental state. Was he a man without a conscience? Was it Dr. Jekyll and Mr. Hyde? Psychiatrists and other professionals of mental health might argue the points, but to the average member of the community on Rock Springs Road, Jim Mallard was just plain mean.

Jim burned the corncribs and discovered that his relatives were wealthy. Where they acquired such wealth is impossible to know now. Jim pondered it only briefly. It wasn't important to him where it originated. He was only interested in how it could end up in his pocket. Jim began spending more time with his aunt and uncle. He learned to cook and prepared their meals. He also took on the role of physician and prescribed an assortment of remedies. Nell Edmondson, their caregiver, grew suspicious and started bringing her own flour for biscuits. Anything she could bring from the garden she used to keep Jim's meals and remedies from making it to the table. But despite her efforts, the elderly couple came under his sinister care.

Jim lived within walking distance of his aunt and uncle in a two-story clapboard house hosting an assortment of residents. He lived with his brother, Mathias, and his sister, Etta. There was also a young couple living with him. All of these people living in only two bedrooms eventually led to sexual advances upon the women. Jim's nickname was Beauty and he had a host of male friends, so the women were at least safe with him. Eventually Jim reduced his affections to only one man, Jesse. Mathias, on the other hand, expanded his repertoire. His inappropriate advances led to his being asked to leave to a nearby community.

In his brother's absence, Jim returned his attention to his aunt and uncle. The medications increased, and the elderly couple's health decreased. Mathias figured out what Jim was doing, so he decided to move closer to keep an eye on his elderly relatives. The night he planned to move to a small home near his brother, it strangely burned down. Everyone knew it was Jim's hand at work.

Day by day Jim tightened the noose. He served meals made with spoiled meat since the old couple could hardly detect the flavors anymore. He increased the medicine dosages prescribed by Doctor Gordon, my great uncle. Then he concocted his own drugs. He was growing impatient. Finally one morning he gave his aunt a double dose of pills. By nine o'clock, she had convulsions and died. Nell, horror-stricken, ran out of the house and never returned. She was a black woman, and in rural Tennessee in those days, there was nothing she could do. No one would ever believe her word over his.

Left alone in the room, Jim closed his aunt's eyes, coldly walked to her desk, and pulled out the forged will he had prepared in substitute, leaving him her part, amounting to about $9000. Then he went to the back parlor where his uncle was resting. Always the actor, Jim sadly informed him of the untimely death of his sister.

Uncle Sam started to put two and two together, so a couple of days later at his sister's funeral he asked JP Gordon, my great-grandfather, to make out a new will for him. JP agreed to do so the next week. Jim found out about it, and two days later prepared a special meal of cooked oysters for his Uncle Sam's supper. Of all his dishes, everyone talked about the oysters. He only served these at picnics and special occasions, so Uncle Sam looked longingly on these rare delicacies. Jim served them to him and left for the evening. When he returned Uncle Sam was dead. As in the case with Aunt Nancy, no autopsy was performed. The will was read, and Jim was left more than $20,000. Mathias, his brother, received only a dollar.

Actually, Jim had been preparing this for a long time. He copied a will from the *Saturday Evening Post* and forged all of the information on it. He found two witnesses. One was an elderly man who was dying of old age. The other was a fifteen-year-old boy whom he later poisoned. There was no one left to verify the authenticity of the will, but Jim's other two aunts contested the will and won. In the end, Jim only received eighty acres and a thousand dollars. His aunts, Molly and Sue, received the remainder.

Jim had accrued debts from fast living, so he sold some of the land to my great-grandfather. He also gave the rest to Jesse, his lover, for "love and a dollar." In this he hoped to keep from losing all of his assets. Jim knew he could count on Jesse to launder his money for him until the appropriate time when Jesse would give it back.

At this time, Jim invited Aunt Sue to live with him. He told her there were no grudges about her challenging the will. He wanted to let bygones be bygones. Since he had no children of his own, he explained that he wanted to care for her and the remaining members of his family just as he had for his dead aunt and uncle. She accepted the invitation and moved in. Jim wined and dined her for months, including his specialty, cooked oysters. Aunt Sue started showing signs of fatigue. He treated her with his remedies and convinced her he knew more than the doctors. Shortly, she died of convulsions. Again, there was no autopsy.

At Sue's funeral, Jim asked Aunt Molly if she wanted to come live with him. He assured her he would care for her as he had for her sister. She outright refused and accused him of having something to do with her death. That night Jim burned down the barn on her property, and for no reason he burned Nell Edmondson's abandoned home. Jim Mallard's life was spinning out of control.

The Mallard house was now occupied by Jim, Mathias, Etta, Jesse, and an array of young boys. Jim fixed the boys a pot of hot chocolate one morning, and they became extremely sick. No one died, but the boys moved out. Even teenagers figure out some things on their own. Jesse realized how mentally ill Jim was. Jim also began to doubt Jesse's faithfulness, so he demanded his assets to be returned. Jesse refused. For once in his life, Jim was at an impasse, but only briefly. It was simple. It had worked many times before. Murder was his ultimate solution.

Jim planned to shoot Jesse in the upstairs room where they slept together. Then he planned to return downstairs and shoot his sister Etta, who spent her evenings preparing food for the next day. His brother, Mathias, was an invalid by now, the result of an accident involving Jim, so he planned to set the house on fire, knowing that Mathias couldn't get out. With everyone dead, Jim would once again forge a will and get his property back.

The appointed night arrived. Jim eased up the stairway with a pistol concealed in his pocket. He slipped into bed with Jesse, who was already asleep. And he waited. Etta was finishing the dishes in the kitchen, and Mathias was resting in the parlor where he spent most of his day. It was a very cold evening, and Jesse had piled several quilts and blankets over him. The bedroom grew deathly still. Jim pulled out his pistol and, pressing it to the blankets, fired one shot. The quilt muffled the sound. Jesse never budged.

Without hesitation, Jim descended the stairs where he found Etta in the kitchen as predicted. He shot her at point-blank range, and she collapsed unconscious on the floor. Jim locked all of the doors so Mathias couldn't get out, but then he remembered that Jesse had made no movement when he was shot, so he went back upstairs. When he entered their bedroom, Jesse was standing behind the door holding the bullet that only penetrated the blankets, but not him.

"Beauty, what's the meaning of this?" Jesse asked. Then both men sat down on the bed, Jim with a smoking gun, and Jesse with the bullet. They sat there for some time, discussing the basics of a good relationship. Finally, Jesse went downstairs where he found Etta. He called the ambulance and the sheriff. Jim offered no resistance. Etta was taken to the hospital, where she died two weeks later, and Jim was taken to jail.

The trial took place at the courthouse. Dr. Farmer, from the state asylum, interviewed Jim and found him insane, but the lawyers changed the charge to second-degree murder because they couldn't profit as much on a plea of insanity. During the trial, Jim confessed to everything with a nonchalant attitude, telling the details as if telling a story to children. His only animated moment came when he remembered that Jesse owed him for the farm. Jesse had anticipated this and had already sold it to my grandfather.

Investigators found a ladder outside leading to the upstairs window of Jim's bedroom, but no conclusion was made to its purpose. They searched for the pistol, but to no avail. Some thought he threw it down the well, but again nothing was found. Questions arose to the apparent ignorance of the family and the community at the sequence of these strange events. No one intervened. Much like the Salem Witch Trials, no one could remember how it all started. Like a bad dream, everyone woke up, dismissed the whole thing, and went back to work.

Jim Mallard went to the state prison for forty or so years. As remarkable as it may seem, the man who poisoned an uncle and two aunts, who shot and killed his sister, who poisoned a young boy, who attempted the poisoning of several others, who prepared to burn down the house with his brother inside, and who attempted to kill his lover, was eventually released. He returned to our farm and demanded ownership. One of our hired hands was there alone and informed Jim that the Gordon family now owned all of the land. Jim immediately turned, got in his car, and no one ever saw him again in the area.

Until recently, I had no idea where any of the Mallards were buried except Mathias. His tombstone sat between two barns my father built in the late fifties. As the farm expanded, more room was necessary, so we moved the headstone near a pond where it sat neglected for years. Eventually the headstone was moved to the Gordon Cemetery so the story would never die. It is the only visible evidence of a series of strange events that hardly seem at home on Rock Springs Road. But this tale didn't end with Jim Mallard's death. Decades later, his ghost revisited our farm in a strange and eerie way. He returned in a form that took me off guard. The monster slipped out of a cabinet one evening, leaving an imprint on me forever.

CHAPTER
NINE

A baker's dozen is thirteen, owing to the generosity of the culinary guild, but a farm boy's dozen years is more like eight, owing to his isolation from the world, keeping his innocence intact. When I was twelve years old, my world was Camelot, where chivalrous men protected the honor of women, where virtue guided men's actions, and every discovery led to beauty. I did not believe in shadows. But the world does not wait for us to grow up and learn about the dark things; it grows us up, sometimes abruptly, whether we are ready or not. The dark clouds of reality were rolling in.

With the regular farming day completed, I walked down the long lane leading to the old abandoned Mallard house. It was still discussed by the old timers as the locale of a series of killings in the 1920s. The alfalfa field lay to my right. A dilapidated old barn that would later be dismantled and moved to the pioneer village, Cannonsburgh, and falsely referred to as the Gordon School lay to the left behind a sprawling oak tree. At the end of the lane, positioned among an ancient pear tree and flanked by two stone fireplaces, stood the Mallard house. In the spring, it was an island among a sea of daffodils. These flowers were an enduring sign of previous homesteaders' commitments to beauty as it played into the daily struggle for survival. Although the Mallard house continued to deteriorate yearly, reminding us we were only yet another generation building things that would eventually fall into disrepair, the resurgence of yellow each spring whispered that we were not alone.

This particular evening I entered the old house to look around and imagine the events that gave it its notoriety. I saw old Jim Mallard creeping up the stairs to do his business, and then slithering back down to kill someone else. I moved about the house, recreating the crime with an uncontrolled imagination. I tried desperately to warn Mathias, but he couldn't hear me. I heard Jim coming. Passing through the kitchen, I urged Etta to leave, then she was on the floor in a pool of blood. Jim turned and looked dead into my eyes. I ran to the nearest cabinet and opened it to grab a gun to put an end to Jim for good.

Instead, a magazine fell out. I had never seen a naked woman before, and this one had pictures of lots of them. My heart pounded, and I flipped through page after page. My head started spinning, and I felt like I was suffocating. I grew nauseous, ran outside, and threw up. Then I returned to flip through more pages. I had seen many cows' udders in my short life, but this was different. Seconds turned into minutes until I was exhausted. I was weak as I returned slowly back to my home.

For several evenings, like a dog returning to its vomit, I made my way back down the lane, which slowly turned into a dark, narrow tunnel shutting out the beauty on either side. Going there was like sliding down a waterfall of excitement. Returning home was the climbing of a very steep mountain laced with shame and dishonesty. A rush of emotion propelled me each night, blinding me and isolating me from the world I knew and loved. The loss of innocence was at first exhilarating, and the guilt was never strong enough to diminish the evening journey. Then, little by little, it choked the life out of me. The images branded on my mind at night flashed in a steady stream all day. I hated the very thing I revisited each evening. And I began to hate myself.

Then one evening the cabinet was empty. The pictures were gone. I assumed the hired hand, John, had collected them. I wept out of relief. Without his knowing it, John did for me what I could not do for myself. I thanked him silently. Standing in the same kitchen where several people were killed fifty years before, I nearly joined their ranks, emotionally speaking. But I survived. My character, which should have been the antidote, had failed me. I understood for the first time that I was made of clay. I left by the same doorway that evening that old Jim Mallard was escorted out and sent to prison years before, but I walked out a free man.

Standing on the front porch at dusk, I noticed the vibrant yellows of the daffodils. The alfalfa was in bloom, a deep purple, and the sunset sprayed its colors across the sky. The lane was level again, perhaps a bit downhill as I returned home on lighter feet. But I was different. I felt the weariness of having aged too much, too soon. Those images still haunt me many years later, and when I think of the youth of my sons, the weariness returns as I consider that a Mallard house sits in every computer, ready to spill out into their hearts. With the strike of a key, the lane is walked, the cabinet opened, and John isn't there to take it away.

John had a bride of sixteen; he was in his mid-thirties. They both looked fifty. He told me once he didn't allow the girl to get out of bed each morning until he returned to her from the morning milking. He spoke as one who bags a trophy or notches a gun. She had huge brown eyes, sad and strained. She rarely spoke and had a peculiar habit of wrapping her arms around herself. I only had one conversation with her. She was leaning against the back porch post that day as I approached. She was thin, but dignified. Her voice was tired, but hopeful. She greeted me casually, but as we talked, she kept staring off into the distance at a bend in the creek, eyeing it as if she was creating her own world. She occasionally looked toward me, but never directly at me. We never really made eye contact. Eventually, I walked away as she continued her fascination with something I could not see. I never saw her again on the back porch. She disappeared. Within the year, she was with child. John lost interest in farming, so he packed up his few possessions, including his wife, and drove out of our lives.

After a hired hand moved out of one of our tenant houses, we had the unenviable job of preparing it for the next occupant. We never knew what to expect. One tenant, years before, had actually dismantled the house to use as firewood. He was literally burning the house down from the inside. Another one stored all of his trash in one room, which was full after only a year. We entered the house expecting the worst. Instead, we were shocked to discover several beautiful murals drawn full length across the walls. We stood mesmerized. Somehow, between the incessant sex demanded of her, this beautiful young girl found time to exercise the gift of her art. Centermost was a river flowing through a paradise, perhaps something that took her away. Her images exuded happiness. They were bright colors, lots of yellows like the daffodils in the Mallard yard, and immediately I thought of the nude women I had gazed upon just a month before. I wondered how many of them aspired to be artists, how many had dreams of music or poetry. For some reason I felt responsible just for being male.

We whitewashed the walls, covering up a young girl's fantasy world. With each stroke of new paint, her memory faded. We removed all traces of her masterpiece. Two weeks later, the next hired hand arrived. He drove up in a dilapidated piece of junk. He got out, and the rest of the family positioned themselves behind him. He introduced himself, and as an afterthought, introduced his so-called old lady, who could have been misconstrued as a teenager except that she had four children at her side. When he turned and eyed her, she cowered at his glare and retreated back inside the car with the children. Another saga began on Rock Springs Road, and I realized that summer that Camelot was only a myth.

CHAPTER TEN

The next year brought more trips down to the Mallard house, but this was for the sole purpose of starting my own business venture as a budding entrepreneur. I was thirteen years old when my father financed my first mule with a hundred and fifty dollars. It came with four legs, paper-thin skin, and a long sad face. Ancient, I named him Methuselah. Mules are uniquely hybrid and sterile, so that if all the mules on the planet died, they would escape extinction as soon as the first jack—a male donkey—bred a mare and a foal appeared. So Methuselah knew nothing of romance, explaining the sad face, but his was sadder and longer than most due to his long, toilsome life.

Fifty years before, mules held a distinguished place of honor on the farm and were treated with respect because they provided the energy to produce the vast quantities of goods necessary for the family's existence. But with the advent of the tractor, the mule fell out of favor, and subsequent generations regarded him with disdain and those associated with him as backward. The mule lost his posh position in the barn and was left to fend for himself in overgrazed pastures. Such was the plight of Methuselah, but with whatever life he had left in him, he was my ticket to financial security as I prepared that spring to raise tomatoes.

Tomatoes during Shakespeare's day were assumed poisonous and were used as projectiles hurled at bad actors in the Globe Theater. A hit to the mouth was thought to bring a quick death, which was not altogether a myth. In Elizabethan England, the wealthy ate many of their meals, including tomatoes, on pewter plates containing high levels of lead that leeched out in the presence of the acidic tomato. The poor, who ate on wood, escaped the hazard. Thus, fine dining became lethal, and the tomato took the rap. The upstanding members of society pronounced a guilty verdict, and the tomato would not regain its popularity for a couple of hundred years. It finally caught on in this country at the end of the nineteenth century with the invention of the American pizza, and the tomato's popularity has soared ever since, or at least that was what I was banking on.

I planted a hundred tomato plants, staked them with old sticks, and tied them to the stakes with leftover, discarded panty hose. When the first weeds appeared, I proudly hooked up my Old Testament friend to a rusty harrow and made war. He was even older than I thought. When he got to the end of the row on the first pass, he just stood there. No amount of coaxing convinced him the job was not completed. Eventually, on his schedule, he slowly turned and plodded down the second row, but this entirely exhausted his reserve tank. Taking pity, I unhooked and led him back to his pasture where he died that night.

As the dead wagon pulled out of our driveway the following day, thoughts of my younger sister harnessed to the harrow, making good my business venture, faded away as I remembered what the exploitation had done to Methuselah. She was, after all, my sister. I did mention it to her, but the glare I received made me think she thought there was still more room on the dead wagon. Having spent a hundred and fifty dollars for a dead mule, I became, by default, the ass, and I weeded those tomatoes religiously each evening after my work on the farm was completed.

I enjoyed working in the evenings by myself. The isolation fit my personality, which I was told was textbook introvert. I disagree. Introverts gather strength from being alone. I, however, have never been alone. I always have myself and thoroughly enjoy spending time with me. I talk aloud to myself, and if the noise gets too much, I talk to myself in silence. So I worked on those tomatoes in solitary company.

The rain came, the tomatoes prospered, and my ship came in. The bounty exceeded my expectations, with the first picking yielding 200 pounds. They looked and smelled like tomatoes, but they were money to me. Too young to drive, I begged my sister-in-law to haul my tomatoes in her green Pinto to local stores. We delivered our first tomatoes to Brown's Grocery. Mr. Brown was as colorful as his name, but he received my tomatoes with enthusiasm and paid me fifty cents a pound.

Three days later saw another hundred and fifty pounds, but upon delivery, Mr. Brown's excitement waned, and he offered me twenty-five cents a pound. Stunned, I took the money, a 50-percent reduction, but I knew my profit margin still existed, albeit small. By the end of the week, the tomatoes were still producing heavily, but when I arrived at the store, I perceived a red glow pulsing from the windows. Apparently I did not represent a monopoly, and everyone was selling tomatoes with few buyers. He reluctantly offered a nickel a pound.

My mule was dead. My surplus crop had no subsidies. My free transportation insisted on gas reimbursements and was reticent about receiving tomatoes as payment-in-kind. In short, I was broke. In long, I was very broke. The remainder of the summer we ate a lot of tomatoes on lead-free plates. With the excess, I started a compost pile in the corner of the garden, and I began to learn about turning waste into something beautiful and useful.

Methuselah taught me a valuable lesson. You can't depend on mules or sisters, so I became a supporter of the Industrial Revolution and purchased my first Troy-Bilt rototiller. Gardening became a hobby. The law of supply and demand began and ended with my appetite, and the value placed on the food I grew was measured by the complete satisfaction I received, mouthful by mouthful.

CHAPTER ELEVEN

Boredom is strictly a state of mind. With the right attitude, the common day's activities on the farm become exciting challenges. Often my imagination made a world-class event out of the dreariest of jobs. One of these involved the feeding of twenty sows near the old Mallard house. I fed them in a series of containers made from hot water heaters cut in half to form semicircular troughs. Nothing was wasted then. I carried two five-gallon buckets full of ground corn down the lane to a small lot where the sows basked in a muddy pond. If they didn't hear my approach, I called them.

My voice had not fully changed to manhood as I entered my fourteenth year. I could hit a high pitch that carried all over the farm. Every farmer has his own word or phrase with his own unique note his animals grow accustomed to. Mine was a suey-peg with a raised inflection on the end of suey resembling a French dignitary. I was very proud of my accent. It wouldn't be until after I dropped French one and my high school German teacher advised me to stick with English that I gave up on foreign languages altogether.

Sows are natural baritones, but when they are excited, their voices instantaneously acquire soprano status. My voice trilled in similar fashion, and they came on the run and lined up in front of the troughs, speaking to one another in dignified operatic voices about the weather or the price of sausage and other pleasantries. I poured out the crushed corn as fast as I could, giving all of them a position at the table for breakfast. Then their dignity gave way and, as hunger will do, reduced them to hogs with hog-like behavior.

My mother said I ate like a pig, but I had watched pigs eat and there were distinct differences. They used their mouths like front-end loaders, scooping up a full load of the corn mash. Then, elevating their massive heads above their bodies, they choked the feed down while gasping for air, which was considerably wasteful, but time saving. At the same time, they squealed and bit each other. I, on the other hand, kept my head down slightly beneath my shoulders and used a fork to shovel my food in with little waste. It was true that I made similar sounds and sometimes my mouth was so full I had to come up for air, but I never bit my sisters. Anyway, I fed the sows, and then the fun began.

Pigs have corkscrew tails, twisting and spiraling upon their backside, resembling those cute buns that many girls with long hair tie up and put pins through. Sows do it without any pretension, but it has the same effect of making them more attractive. If I tried to straighten the tail, it stayed briefly, and then became a curlicue again. The length of time it took for different sows' tails to kink again depended on their dispositions. The more hoggish sows, the ones who were never content with their swill in life, had a quicker return to curl. Their uptight personality manifested itself in their tails, like people whose panties are always in a wad. Everyone needs someone to help him take the kink out of his tail. This is the primary function of marriage.

My objective as they devoured their meal was to straighten each tail with the ultimate goal of having all the tails on all the sows straight at the same time. Ed Sullivan had an act on his show where a man balanced spinning plates on tiny sticks of wood. He spun the first plate and proceeded down the line, returning up and down frantically as some of the plates lost speed and almost fell. Finally all of the plates were spinning simultaneously, and the audience applauded this absurd waste of time. But my plates were pigs, not stationary like the man's sticks. This was much more difficult, and day after day I attempted the impossible.

The previous fall, before I became obsessed by this challenge, my sights were much lower. Our white Yorkshire sows had few hairs on their backs, and their pink skin was visible at a distance. If a sow had a louse, it could be seen scurrying over her back, making busy a humdrum life. I prided myself in picking the lice from the sows' arched backs, casting them to the ground, and crushing them with my boot. These lice were not like human lice or nits that are very small and difficult to see; these were as large as cockroaches. Their massive size diminished the challenge, and shortly I grew bored with the ease with which I could strip all the lice from the backs of all the sows while they ate. So I moved on.

On the farm as well as in other walks of life, ordinary days are sufficient in themselves for the production of extraordinary ones, but because we expect so little of a day and rarely expect the unexpected, we trounce upon diamonds looking for glass. The sows came on the run, lined up for chow, and began inhaling their breakfast. I unconsciously made my way up and down the row, going through the routine of straightening the tails, and then it happened. I froze. All the tails on all the sows pointed down, and ecstasy welled up inside me. One moment, one split second, and the image was gone.

I looked around to see if anyone else had seen it, but the audience had disappeared. After months of dedication, eons of waiting and hoping, striving for the impossible, it happened, and there was no one to congratulate me. The only sounds were a quiet breeze and the slobbering hum of sows. So I congratulated myself on accomplishing something rather remarkable. And I triumphed alone.

Few ever know the countless successes we experience each day. No one appreciates the kind words said in passing or the silent pat on the back. No audience applauds as we gallantly go about saving little birds that have fallen from nests or removing pesky lice from hogs' backs. But if God knows the plight of each sparrow as it falls, then He also knows the joy I received from this ordinary event and, for some reason, it mattered.

The ultimate and practical goal in this exercise, however, came together in the fall. Traditionally, Thanksgiving Day arouses a myriad of senses: the smell of basted turkey, dressing, sweet potato casserole, and the sounds of children playing together while adults discuss politics or watch football. On Rock Springs Road it was different: the smell of smoldering firewood and scorched hair, the sound of rifle then death, and the sight of blood and guts in a serene setting. We all looked forward to this holiday. It was hog-killing day.

The Mitchells hosted the event each year on their farm. I anticipated it for weeks, much as I awaited Christmas. To see a group of men gather from various parts working on a single goal defined community. They came, and they brought their hogs with them, which were unloaded in a small pen. For identification, farmers notched the ears of their hogs much like a brand used on cattle, but it wasn't really necessary in this setting. Even in a pen of twenty hogs, each farmer knew his own because everyone recognizes members of his own family.

The scalding vat, resembling an open-topped metal coffin, was brought out of storage and placed over a shallow pit filled with firewood that acted as a heat source to heat the water in the vat. The heat was maintained at a particular temperature just below boiling. The experienced men gauged the intensity of the heat simply by feeling it with their fingertips. The only purpose of the hot water was to loosen the hair on the hog so it could be scraped off with knives. It was like giving a very large man a shave, and when it was finished, the white hide glistened. The hog need only a little aftershave to make it irresistible.

A long beam was placed between the crotches of two trees to act as a support for the hanging carcasses. The boom hitched to the back of the tractor sat idle beside the pen of hogs, waiting its turn in the process. The rifle barrel was cleaned, the knives sharpened, and by early morning the hogs began arriving from neighboring farms.

Most of the farmers brought their own knives, and there was always discussion about the quality of each and the stories associated with them. My grandfather's was unimpressive, but everyone remembered the year he attempted to cut a hog's jugular and drove the knife through his hand between the bones. He calmly showed those around him the peculiar sight of a knife sticking through his hand. He was taken to the hospital and returned before noon, hand bandaged, to continue the work. After that, his knife had Jim Bowie's reputation, straight from the Alamo.

Hogs are not pigs, which is what everyday people think about when oink and pink come into a conversation. Pigs are cute and make snuggly stuffed animals that sleep with our children. They show up in Disney movies, and are particularly endearing when they are pot-bellied. A hog, on the other hand, is a large shaggy beast with a large head that supports a massive snout that drools constantly. Its narrow beady eyes resemble something demonic, making it easier to kill.

The process started in the pen of hogs. Two men eased in, slowly making their way among them until one hog was isolated. Then the man with the rifle lowered his gun to within inches of the head. The hog's curiosity raised its snout, sniffing the barrel, the trigger was pulled, and the shell was lodged comfortably within the brain. The hog was immediately rendered unconscious and collapsed to the ground. The other man quickly stuck the hog, meaning he cut the jugular so that the blood flowed freely from the body as the heart continued to pump for a short while. Getting rid of the blood played an important role in having the meat at its best.

At this point, the tractor with the boom was backed next to the pen. A man wedged a gambrel stick, narrowed at each end and about two feet long, between the hog's hind legs through the Achilles tendons. The hog was then lifted by the boom. Fully extended, some hogs were about eight feet long. The hog was then transported to the hot water vat and dumped in. The vat had two chains in the water, so the entire hog could be rolled like a rotisserie. After a minute or so, the hog was rolled out onto a flat surface where the men frantically scraped and pulled the hair off. Now the hog resembled the beloved pig and possessed more sex appeal than the barbers who had worked on him.

Again the hog was hoisted by the boom and taken to the large beam positioned about eight feet in the air. One side of the gambrel stick was taken out of the Achilles tendon and, with a mighty lift from a couple of men, the hog was placed on the beam so that it hung head down, swinging free and clear.

Now the older, experienced men took over. Most of these were black men who knew how to extract everything from a hog. They were masters of their trade. They wielded their knives, making effortless strokes that appeared almost like poetry to me. Piece by piece rolled out of the carcass until nothing remained but the hide. It's hard to imagine the variety of meats that come from a hog: sweetbread (kidney), chitterlings (intestines), brains (especially good on scrambled eggs), feet, stomach, liver, and, of course, the snout.

The factory-type process continued all day, and by evening there was a long row of carcasses hanging neatly on the beam. It was such a beautiful sight, such symmetry. We never really thought of it in any other way. From here, they would be moved into the Mitchell shop, cut up and salted down. Weather patterns were so predictable then that it always froze on Thanksgiving Day, keeping the meat safe from spoilage.

My grandfather collected as much fat as he could carry in a washtub from the trimmings and took it to his home in Versailles. I went with him and spent the night. The next day, I found myself standing next to a large cauldron watching a very old black lady stir the fat over the fire. My grandfather shared the spoils with her, and she knew just what to do. She was tall and thin. She smiled at me and quietly sang while she stirred. Occasionally she scraped the bottom of the vat and pulled up what she called cracklings. It was just fried fat. She passed the large wooden spoon in my direction, inviting me to give it a try. I trusted her totally, and I peeled it off and bit in to the most delicious bacon-like Southern food imaginable. Eating this delicacy, stirred by this wonderful lady in my grandfather's backyard, made being young worthwhile.

Whether we understood it or not, we practiced the art of community. Hogs were only the catalyst. Men are accused of poor communication skills, but on hog-killing day the sound of laughter and talking was full and invigorating. It was a very large and vibrant man-cave. This event is not likely to return in my lifetime, but I am thankful I still have the scalding vat in my barn and my grandfather's knife in the shop as reminders of our community and the enjoyment we had in doing this holiday together.

CHAPTER
TWELVE

Veterinary science captures the imagination of most children, especially if they are raised on a farm. During my childhood, we had cattle, chickens, pigs, goats, rabbits, horses, raccoons, cats, and dogs. It was not unusual on any given day to encounter any number of diseases that required the expertise of our veterinarian, but because he always came with a fee, we often tried home remedies with the occasional success. With all the experience of being fifteen years old, I felt very confident in my ability to accurately appraise any malady in any species and deliver a life-saving treatment. Of all the outstanding remedies I performed, the one I am most remembered for in my family is the treatment of Susie, our long-nosed Chihuahua.

Susie displayed chronic wheezing, and my father asked me to take a look at her. I palpated Susie, squeezing her tiny body from head to tail, but I could find nothing unusual like a tumor or something else I knew nothing about. Externally, everything looked great except that she was a Chihuahua, which I despised. She barked at inappropriate times and bit the ankles of unsuspecting visitors. She had actually turned on me a number of times. Susie had a sinister grin and a relatively long nose, which her beady eyes looked down arrogantly, like eyeing down the barrel of a gun. Her short, stubby legs reminded me that her evolutionary journey from a snake had not been so far in the distant past.

As much as I disliked her, the fact remained that she was sick, and it was my appointed job to heal her. I went to the refrigerator and pulled out a bottle of penicillin. When all else fails, pull out the penicillin. The directions indicated that the accurate dosage was two cc's per hundred pounds of bodyweight. Susie weighed about five pounds. The math came out to be one tenth of one cc. I was a proponent of the proven medical adage that if a little is good, a lot is better. Memories of Susie snarling and nipping at my heels loomed before me, and I remembered the times I tried to kick her away, but she was too quick, and that grin, that evil grin smirked at me each time I missed her.

But now she was mine, and I looked into those eyes that didn't look so confident now. She gazed at me as if to say, *I was just kidding*. I could feel her heart beating beneath her black coat. It became a nuisance. In the name of science and for the benefit of mankind, I took the needle and slowly and with deadened responsibility drew out five cc's, fifty times the normal dosage. *That should do it*, I said to myself, *one way or the other*. Having nothing to lose since she represented no financial advantage to the farm or my father, I injected the life-giving serum. If she lived, I would be a hero, if not, I was certain no investigation of foul play would take place.

Susie passed from this world quickly, and rigor mortis set in amazingly soon. Her eyes were huge as they stared dead ahead. Her legs bolted straight down. She was pickled, and we could have put her on the mantle for posterity. Everyone offered their condolences. "I did what I could," I said, and I meant it. We buried her that afternoon.

Then the haunting dreams came. Susie, grinning on the pillow beside me at bedtime, her white teeth gleaming in the full moonlight. Those eyes glaring at me with less mercy than I had shown her. I was beginning to regret my medical decision as I sensed condemnation from the family. I felt their eyes on me. Finally one evening at the supper table when I could bear it no longer, I nonchalantly revealed how sorry I was that the five cc's didn't work. Everyone stopped eating and stared down their long noses at me just like Susie. I could almost hear them snarling. Ginger, who loved Susie the most, got up from the table and went to the refrigerator. I expected her to draw out a thousand cc's for my immediate termination, but she returned with only a glass of water. I was stunned at how casually everyone received the news. "A bit steep," my father said. "But I know you did your best" ("because you are an honorable man," Marc Antony echoed). I didn't finish my supper and asked to be excused. My father consented and said nothing more, but I knew he knew; he always knew. I never again used my professional knowledge to end the life of an animal, not even a Chihuahua. I visited her grave a few times out of guilt. Once I thought of digging her up just to see if, indeed, she had been preserved, but I couldn't bear seeing those cold, steel eyes again. The nightmares subsided, and shortly I regained my dignity as protector of the innocent.

It was at this same time I began raising rabbits for "fun and profit" as the book said. It was great fun, but I don't remember the profit part. I purchased a solid black Flemish Giant doe and named her Martina Luther King. She was a true beauty, and I was very proud of her. She had a large roll of skin just under her chin called a dewlap, and she resembled an overweight nanny. I housed her in an outdoor pen we had used to raise raccoons years before. The plan was to breed her to a solid white Flemish Giant buck, but the first time I put them together, the buck killed her. I was heartbroken, so I named him James Earl Ray and promptly cut his head off.

There were times, however, when a mating was successful, and the pen was crawling with beautiful hairless babies groping around in their mother's fur that she had pulled out to provide a warm home. Even in the animal world, a mother pulls her hair out because of her offspring. I remember one litter came out of its nesting box at night and crawled around on the screen floor. Unfortunately, a dog reached up from the bottom and pulled some of them partially through. The next morning when I came to feed them, there were babies and half-babies hanging beneath the pen.

We were all horrified. Ginger, Teresa, and I decided to give them a proper burial.

We took a shoebox and put the remains in, sealed it, and prepared for the long procession to the cemetery, which was a large pile of rocks in the middle of the field behind the house where Susie was entombed. Ginger thought it appropriate to sing, so we decided on *The Old Rugged Cross*. "On a hill faraway…" we began, and we sang verse after verse with increased emotion. Grieving, we hardly noticed the change in weather. The sky darkened, the wind blew, and Golgotha loomed before us. The more ominous it became the faster we walked, and the hymn turned into a rap. With great haste, we dug a deep hole and deposited the remains. Lightning crashed around us and we broke into a run. I had only taken a few steps when I stopped abruptly and turned around to stare at Susie's grave. I fully expected to see my first resurrection.

I continued raising rabbits for many years, along with catfish, bees, and earthworms, but none of these represented those special farm animals we regarded as having personalities like Emerson Boozer, our German shepherd, my boyhood dog. He was my shadow, my confidant, my counselor, and my friend. We took long walks together, and when we stopped for a short respite, we conversed eye to eye. I was eighteen when he died, and I buried him under the maple tree where he always waited for me. I cried like I had lost my best friend, which I had. Then there was Chigger, the obstinate Shetland pony. Appropriately named, this parasite always ran under low-hanging tree branches in an attempt to brush me off his back. When he died, I happily dragged his carcass to the back of the farm for buzzard consumption.

I mentioned the raccoons. My father took them out of a nest, brought them home, and placed them on a nursing cat that already had three kittens. The kittens died, but the momma cat raised the four raccoons. The one we kept enjoyed sitting on my shoulders at meals, reaching out to get my food as I ate. I took a bite, then offered him some on the same spoon. My immunity was ironclad. We also had hundreds of cats, most dying from disease or from being chopped up by truck motor fans on cold mornings. Cats always seemed expendable to me.

Hardly considered pets, chickens occupied a major part of the farm for many years. My father had four hen houses with a total of 4800 layers. Eggs were collected three times a day, every day. Thousands of eggs daily to wash, sort by size, put in egg cartons, and store in a freezer until we could load them in a pick-up and haul them to local stores. When Momma hauled these to town, she also did the grocery shopping for us, so we went with her. Often, she took all five of us. I was always on the side between her and the door while the other four occupied the rest of the seat. It was tight. One day we rounded a sharp turn and the door on my side popped open. As I fell toward the road, Momma grabbed me just as my head hit the gravel road. A few pebbles were lodged beneath the skin, but she pulled me back up without stopping the truck.

The chickens roosted on structures built in the shape of a gabled roof with wire over the top. The manure fell down through the wire, piling up into huge mounds by springtime. Then we removed the chickens and the structures so we could clean out the manure to be hauled as fertilizer to the fields. As the tractor with a front-end loader scooped the manure, hundreds of rats scattered, and I chased them down, clubbing and piling them up until there was an impressive mound of dead rats by the end of the day. My pile of dead rats was, to me, more impressive than the great trophies of elk or deer heads hunters place in their homes. These hunters have expensive rifles, traveling expenses, costly permits, and endless paraphernalia. All of my fun came to me with the use of a simple stick.

I am thankful that I grew up in a time before computers. Nintendo hardly compares to the killing of rats. The long walks I took with my dog through the woods exceed any Tweet. I feel sorry for bored people in restaurants, mindlessly scrolling on their devices simply because they don't have a raccoon on their shoulder with whom to share their meal. We were far too busy caring for animals and people to keep up with the lives of countless acquaintances on Facebook. But the animals themselves taught me a lot about life. They taught me about faithfulness, loyalty, and love, often revealing to me my lack of those qualities. In the end, the animals were only animals, but in the middle, they provided me with a rich childhood, and when our home was overflowing with tension and being an adolescent was just too confusing, I went to them. They were always available, never too busy, never giving advice, just listening, and quite often that was all I needed.

CHAPTER
THIRTEEN

The year after my high school graduation, I put aside college, staying home to work the farm with my father. My brother and sisters had already moved on. A part of me wanted everyone to stay on the farm forever. Even with its anxieties and strained relationships, it was all I knew. The familiarity of the stress expressed itself in an odd contentedness with those I loved and went through life with. But they grew up, left home, and Saturday afternoons were mine alone. Unless a particular job pressed upon us, like chopping silage or sowing wheat, we took Saturday afternoons off until four o'clock, when milking resumed. For four hours, the farm became my solitary kingdom.

Four hundred fifty acres provided ample walking spaces, and I devoured vast tracts in a short time. I ambled at a steady pace, a gentle mixture of my grandfather's gait, who never hurried anywhere, and my father's pace, whose ambitions kept his head downward and propelled him throughout each day's successes. In Raphael's painting, *The School of Athens*, Plato looks upward to the heavens to find meaning in the everyday while Aristotle looks downward to the particulars to understand the eternal. As I strolled across the farm, I felt particularly fortunate in having a Platonic grandfather and an Aristotelian father.

One of my favorite adventures was walking down the lane, past the Mallard house, to the Woods Lot. It was here, years before, that I shot my first squirrel with my father's twenty-gauge shotgun. I rose that day before sunrise so I could position myself near a tree before the squirrels woke. About sunrise, I detected some movement high in a hickory tree. A squirrel's nest is little more than a pile of leaves packed between branches. I saw a small head looking out over the edge of its nest. Carefully I raised my gun until the tiny head came into view just above the sight bead. I pulled the trigger, shattering the nest, and a lifeless object tumbled to the ground. Elation accompanied me as I ran to the base of the hickory where I discovered the mangled remains of a baby squirrel. I glanced up, but there was nothing left of their abode. I carried my trophy to the edge of the woods and buried it. I never hunted squirrels again.

The Woods Lot had recently been thinned, cutting down many of the older walnut trees. My father knew when to harvest trees to maximize profit and allow future trees to grow. My grandfather opposed their cutting altogether. They were divine to him. My father, however, regarded trees as a means to an end. They came down in order to send us to college. The Athenian conflict was forever with us. The cutting left an array of stumps scattered among the survivors. It was upon these stumps I sat in the quiet of the trees and thought. In total silence, my thoughts crowded about me like so many friends. I never experienced loneliness there.

One particular balmy afternoon as I conversed with my thoughts, a new, perplexing idea slipped in unexpectedly between the normal mental processes. Where it originated I did not know. *Had I caught a private conversation between two stumps? Had it fallen from the oak tree on the back of a leaf?* But there it was, and it demanded an audience with my other thought-friends. The image was this: I was in the den of our home talking to God. He was relaxing in the soft LaZ-Boy recliner reserved only for my father. This seemed fitting. I couldn't make out His face as He was hidden behind a large manuscript, poring over a list of projects I planned to incorporate in an attempt at sharing Christ with a fictitious neighbor. This was a strange image because I am not evangelistic, but I am hypothetical because it helps me discover truth.

After a long scrutiny of my list, God informed me that it was a good plan, but then added it wouldn't matter because He knew the neighbor would never accept and believe in Him. With that he disappeared, probably to have tea somewhere with John Calvin. I stared at the list for some time. Then I picked it up, and that perplexing thought entered: *To do or not to do.*

Was it a waste of time to do for someone if it yielded no eternal results? If there is no tangible reward, what's the point? The questions themselves confronted and condemned my legalistic nature. Sadly, I wondered if I had ever really loved anyone at all, just for love's sake. *Was love only an item on a list to be checked off to satisfy the requirements of God's law—a law I had attempted to live because I had no relationship with Him?* My cause-and-effect life seemed so shallow.

In his book *That Man Is You*, Louis Evely tells the story of Judgment Day when, at the end of time, all stand before God. The Lord raises His hand and declares all are forgiven and everyone is welcomed into heaven. At this pronouncement, a man screams out at the injustice of it all. He angrily declares that he sacrificed everything to do His will and now only receives the same reward as everyone else. Then the Lord raises His hand again and says, "Except you."

Was I that man? Strangely, I felt no condemnation. God granted me peace just for being honest with myself, and I felt His good pleasure. But I couldn't come to any decisive conclusion concerning God, in general. I had not spent enough time alone with my stumps, where the voice of reason could adequately debate faith. *Could they be the same?* It started to rain. I looked up, and though I felt empty, I became aware of the energized world around me, full of Someone I wanted to know, personally, Someone who would love an unlovable me, for no reason at all. Sitting on that stump that Saturday afternoon, gazing upward as the rain washed over me, I experienced church with my silent congregation in a new way.

It was a quarter of four and time to leave. I returned to the barn to find a herd of un-milked cows. Sometimes I thought they should do it themselves, but it never happened. This was my tangible world. Reality has its place and offers a bit of security after dreaming, but I still could not entirely leave my questions. As I washed each udder that evening, my mind settled in on Christ on the cross. *Would He have died if His death had brought no one into His kingdom? Did He go to the cross to obtain results or was it strictly a response from a God who is in love with us? Does He ever do anything for any other purpose than just being Himself? Is His love for us ever wasted?*

The milking parlor provided a fertile environment for the extraction of conclusions. The cows listened well and were not judgmental. The regular cadence of the milking machines beat measured and slow, and the barn cats sipped spilt milk at the cows' feet. However, as the last cow exited the barn that night and I washed the last bit of manure down the drain and cut off the lights, I still had no answers. When there are no theological answers, the only practical solution is to return home to a great supper prepared by the hands of someone who loved me, regardless of what I did or who I was. I suppose that was the answer to my questions all along.

When I walked in the house, there she was, my mother, leaning over the stove, cooking supper. My father was in his recliner with his newspaper, exhausted after another long day. There were only three of us now. She called us to supper, and we sat down around the kitchen table to turnip greens, minute steak, mashed potatoes, and cornbread with molasses. We talked about the farm, the animals, and the jobs for the next day. When the dishes were cleared and put away, Momma and I spent time together, and I began to write in the quiet of each evening. Sometimes we watched TV, and my mother's favorite was *The Carol Burnett Show*. At the close of each episode, she sang, "Seems we just get started and before you know it, comes a time we have to say 'so long.'" Little did I realize how soon the song proved true. The next fall I enrolled in Auburn University. Everything present became forever past. It was not just the end of a chapter, it was the final entry in the book of my youth.

The day I drove down our driveway in Grandmother's Chevrolet Biscayne headed for college, I glanced in the rear-view mirror. Momma was standing motionless watching her final child leave home. Daddy was already headed to the barn to tackle the endless work of dairy farming. I hesitated. I wanted to stay. It was at this precise moment I realized I did not know who I was, but I knew from whom I had descended. With a host of witnesses from ages past urging me on, I pushed on the accelerator and turned onto the road where I once dreamed of winning a gold medal.

I passed all of the familiar places. What a silly notion to dream of competing in the Olympics, but that was to be expected when you are fourteen. Now, at nineteen, I knew better. I had matured. I was heading out into the big world to do what adults did. *From now on,* I thought, *I would put away childish things.* Then suddenly the leaves of the corn on that hot August day rose in jubilation. The dust became confetti as I heard the roar of the crowd echoing inside my helmet. The old Biscayne transformed, and I gripped the steering wheel as I raced down the Bonneville Salt Flats, hoping to break a new land speed record.

Between two historic highways in Rutherford County rambles Rock Springs Road. I was born here, and it has been and continues to be my home. I would not trade it for the entire Silk Road. Marco Polo may have delighted Europe with his great treasures from China, but I doubt if he ever straightened out a row of sows' tails. He may have met the Kublai Khan, but he never knew my Catherine the Great. On his thousand-mile trek he may have encountered marauders with dubious stories of intrigue, but he never heard the tale of old Jim Mallard. He may have paddled on the Blue Danube, but he never spent a Saturday afternoon on Dry Fork with my grandfather. I bet Marco Polo never raised tomatoes with a broken-down mule, or knocked the tusks out of a boar's mouth, or piled up stacks of dead rats. Marco Polo was, indeed, a poor man.

I love the road where the people lived who loved me in my youth. Their colorful personalities washed over me, like a watercolor bleeding into a fabric that became me. I am no more than the sum total of their lives. They, like the road itself, wind in and out of me, providing the hard surface on which I have walked through life. It was on this road that I grew up, where I experienced love for no reason, where being alone was never lonely, where I sat at the feet of Catherine the Great, where I walked with Aristotle and Plato, and ran with the notion that dreams were not illusions. It was on this inconsequential byway I rambled in my wonder-years, here on Rock Springs Road.

PART TWO

CHAPTER
FOURTEEN

"Wanna have some fun today?"

The slow, deep voice on the other end of the phone was Mr. Leroy. It was my first year at Auburn University, and he had employed me to do general livestock work. This included feeding hogs, running cattle, and doing any number of odd jobs. The work reminded me of home and helped soothe the continuous empty feeling of homesickness. He never said much, but whenever he used the word fun, it was loaded.

It was Sunday, and the house trailer I rented from him was emptier than usual, so I said I'd love to. I would skip church, but time with Mr. Leroy invigorated the soul. At church, I spent most of the time looking at the back of people's heads, having a negative effect on conversation, and by extension, community. Being with Mr. Leroy was real, and I never wanted to miss anything he said. I looked forward to the two of us spending time together, especially since we spent it face to face.

"What are we doing?" I prodded.

He didn't reply, except to say it was just another odd job. He said he would pick me up in an hour or so. When he arrived, the overcast day had turned into a downpour, so I assumed the event was cancelled, but he waved at me from the truck to come on. I walked out slowly into the rain with just my ball cap on. I never used an umbrella. I sauntered to emphasize that rain was only rain, and I wasn't made of sugar. I didn't chew tobacco, so I had to flaunt my manliness in more creative ways.

When I got in the cab, he said he had been called to pick up a corpse in a back hollow where the washed-out roads made it impossible for the funeral home to go, so they called him with his four-wheel drive flatbed truck. We drove many miles into an area unknown to me. Just when I thought we were at the end of the earth, he turned off the asphalt road onto a sandy loam bed that continued until we turned onto a narrow, clay drive winding down through a grove of pines. The rain was a torrent by now, and the wind was gale force. Mr. Leroy spoke uncharacteristically loudly over the driving rain. His accent was a South Alabama drawl, resembling the beautiful Virginia dialect but without the dignity. He took my name, Gilbert, and crushed it into a slur.

"Gibut, ya ever dipped?"

I had dipped hogs in boiling water at a hog killing. I had dipped small animals as a treatment for fleas. I had even gone skinny-dipping in the pond back home. So I wasn't sure which one he was referring to. He could tell I was confused.

"Have ya ever put a pinch of tobacco between your cheek and gum?"

"Of course not, I don't chew tobacco, Mr. Leroy!"

I never smoked, because coughing wasn't my idea of enjoyment. I never drank because a few of the very special people in my life were alcoholics, and I saw at an early age what it did to them and their families. And chewing tobacco always reminded me of the grasshoppers I used to catch for fishing bait. They foamed up around the mouth with the most disgusting black ooze. I glanced over at Mr. Leroy, but his otherwise jovial face was serious.

"It's Sunday, Gibut. We don't chew tobacco on Sunday; we dip." He said it with such a sense of awe I felt I was on holy ground. He explained there were six days whereby we conducted our lives in everyday ways: making a living, loving our families, caring for our neighbors, and chewing tobacco. But on the Lord's Day, it was different. He talked about dipping snuff like it was communion.

I didn't want to be irreverent, so I consented. He reached in his back pocket and pulled out a can of Copenhagen smoke-less tobacco, what I called snuff. He had dipped for so long that all of his blue jeans had a permanent circular emblem of the can on his rump, which represented a type of badge of honor. I had seen a lot of this at Auburn University in the Animal Science Department. Spittoons in the form of coffee mugs and Styrofoam cups were pervasive in and out of the classroom and denoted prestige. When a boy in the Ag School asked a girl out on a date, she would inconspicuously peer around his backside to make sure he had the manly emblem before she consented. Girls didn't chew, but they only dated boys who did, as the saying went.

"Take a pinch."

I took a small pinch like my mother would have taken applying salt to her cooking. I think I insulted him. He held the can steady, so I took some more, then more. Then I packed it between my cheek and gum. He smiled. I had not known Mr. Leroy long, but I had learned that when he smiled, it meant that God Almighty was pleased. Sometimes his smile was accompanied with squinted eyes, indicating something was about to occur. Another mile down the path, we came to a gate leading into a meadow that we hoped led to our destination. It was still raining heavily.

"Could ya open the gate, Gibut?"

I jumped out, took two steps, and suddenly something strange happened. My ears began to buzz, and my feet felt strangely unsteady. I walked toward the gate, but it avoided me, slowly moving away. My head started spinning, and I found myself on all fours in the mud. I gagged until breakfast found its way out. I finally staggered to my feet and opened the gate. He slowly, very slowly, drove through, what seemed like forever. I shut it and dragged myself back to the cab.

I wasn't aware of Mr. Leroy, but the truck was shaking, and as my head slowly turned toward him, I discovered his huge body vibrating, and I heard him laughing beneath his dignified persona. Mr. Leroy had become my father away from home. He was nothing like my father, as he laughed and told jokes at every opportunity, but he still carried an air of authority. We enjoyed each other's company. He was the kind of man you wanted to have on your side; he was the Alabama version of John Wayne, and he treated me like a son. So his laughter was his way of saying he loved me. We proceeded across a precarious muddy field arriving at our destination.

Many distinguishable artifacts adorned the front yard. Two rusting automobiles on concrete blocks obstructed the muddy pathway leading to the front porch. A huge satellite dish positioned in the middle of the yard made me think someone was trying to communicate with other life forms. Trash, a pile of beer cans, springs from an old bed, and a series of potholes the dogs wallowed in looked like a glorified junkyard.

We approached the cabin slowly, side by side, as one might approach a potential gunfight. Slowly, in the rain, only our caps on, we walked up onto the porch. The matriarch was sitting in a broken-down hickory rocking chair. Mr. Leroy tipped his hat to her, and we entered the house. The tipping of one's hat said that we were gentlemen come to do some good deed. Words seldom accompanied the action.

It was difficult to discern whether the stench we encountered emanated from the dead body or from a host of living ones. Mounds of trash lay in every corner of the front parlor. It appeared the house was abandoned. We walked through the darkened kitchen into a back room where we heard voices and saw a blue haze. We felt our way along the hallway and found ourselves standing in a doorway, looking into the den. The room was packed with family members of various ages and dogs of every description, but they were all doing the same thing, even the dogs: watching a football game.

No one noticed us, so Mr. Leroy tipped his hat. This should have aroused attention, but still no one moved. Then suddenly one team scored, and they all rose to their feet screaming, dogs howling. It was at this point they noticed someone unusual in their midst. No welcome, they just stood and stared.

Mr. Leroy broke the silence. "We've come to pick up the body."

They stared incredulously at us with a peculiar confusion. "So why are you back here, she's on the front porch. You couldn't have missed her." Someone from the back of the room added, "Be careful with the dress, she was married in it." With that announcement, they all settled back into their chairs, and the football game resumed. Mr. Leroy and I looked at each other, but if he had any misgiving about this new revelation, he never let on. He slowly tipped his hat again, and we moved back through the hallway, through the filthy kitchen, and back onto the porch.

They were right. There she was, strapped to the rocking chair, swaying in the wind. What I earlier thought was a handkerchief on her wrist was a small piece of paper pinned to her sleeve with her name on it, as if she were a package to be sent through the mail. Mr. Leroy looked her over carefully. The tobacco was now oozing from the corners of his mouth, meaning he was in deep contemplation. He put his hand on her shoulder and nudged gently. "Damn, she's already stiff in the sittin' position."

I immediately envisioned her in the cab with us, my arm around her to keep her steady. I had never put my arm around a girl in a car or a truck, but I had heard such stories. This, though, lacked the excitement I had imagined. Thankfully, Mr. Leroy had a

different plan, "We'll have to lay her on her side in the truck bed."
I don't know why it made any difference, but he thought it wasn't
dignified having her ride with her knees up.

He grabbed her around the shoulders, and I grabbed her tiny
feet. Then we hoisted her onto the flatbed. I had done this many
times back home on the farm with sacks of feed, but grain doesn't
get stiff, and it never looked at me like she did. We left the cabin
and headed back toward civilization. The rain intensified, and the
small rivulet across one small stream was now a substantial river.
As Mr. Leroy approached it, he hunkered down, and his resolve
became intense. The tobacco was oozing again. He gunned it,
and the truck hit the water, parting it like the Red Sea. It started
fishtailing, making me nervous, but Mr. Leroy was delighted. The
grin on his face reflected success, but when I looked in the rear
view mirror and saw an empty bed, I panicked. "Mr. Leroy, she's
no longer with us."

"I know," he said calmly, "that's the meaning of death."

"No, I mean we lost her in the ditch." He never changed
expressions, but turned the truck around and retraced his tracks.
We found her beside the swollen creek, muddy from head to toe.
This time he grabbed her by the midsection and carefully placed
her back on the truck without my help. Extremely annoyed, he
found a chain behind the driver's seat and secured her to the bed,
crisscrossing her multiple times. She looked like Jacob Marley's
haunting of Scrooge.

We continued the return trip. I didn't look in the rear view
mirror again. I just hoped she stayed put. My mind went back to
my home. This wasn't the way we did things there. I had come to

Auburn University not knowing what to expect. It proved to be a stark awakening. I had never had a class larger than fifteen students in my life, but in my first physics class there were 300. I thought everyone in Alabama was trying to become an engineer. I walked around the perimeter of the school between classes to alleviate the loneliness. I was like those big cats at the zoo who pace the circumference of their cages, hoping something will change or perhaps they will at least be noticed and someone will comment, "Hey, isn't that the king of the beasts?"

I fully expected someone to stop me and say, "Hey, aren't you a Gordon from Rock Springs Road? Is it true that your great grandfather had the first electric lights in the southeastern part of Rutherford County? My father always told me tales of the great Gordon family."

It never happened.

My other claim to fame was I attended Webb School in Bell Buckle, Tennessee. While there, we were told how special we were and that Webb had the prestige of having more Rhodes Scholars than any other secondary school in the South. I thought it was Roads Scholar, like a traveling smart person. Having thought that, it was apparent I wasn't going to be one.

"Hey, I can tell by your brilliant demeanor that you graduated from The Webb School in Bell Buckle Tennessee. Aren't you supposed to be a Rhodes Scholar, like a traveling smart person?"

It never happened.

I was raised on a country road with fewer than fifty people, and I had graduated high school in a class of twenty-five. Now I was surrounded by 20,000 students and none of them knew who I was or where I came from. After several weeks of pacing this university cage, hoping to be recognized, I realized my smallness. Then one day, having grown accustomed to my insignificance, a dear friend walked up beside me and placed her hand in mine. I had not thought of Miss Emily Dickinson in a while, but she whispered gently in my ear, "I'm Nobody, Who are you? Are you Nobody, too?"

Before I could answer she went on, "Then there's a pair of us! Don't tell. They'd banish us you know. How dreary to be Someone, how public like a Frog, to tell one's name the livelong day, to an admiring bog."

It was good to hear her voice again. She had often spoken through my mother. The message was not about smallness, but about importance in a world of self-importance. She and I walked together for a few more days until I regained my stride. Then she returned to Massachusetts, but I knew she was never very far away. It had been difficult leaving home and travelling 300 miles south to this foreign land. I had never been so far away in my life. South Alabama was pines, red clay, and wide-open skies. But in many ways, it was all the same. I had met genuine men like Mr. Leroy, a man I could look up to. I was always content as long as I had someone who kept my compass pointed to due north. I was Somebody to him, and that was enough.

"Gibut, ya hungry?"

Before I could answer, he pulled into the Pines Restaurant, parked near the entrance, and turned the engine off. The rain had diminished to a trickle.

"Maybe we should deliver her to the funeral home before eating," I suggested.

"Two-for-one night and expires at six. They have the best hamburgers around."

We got out of the truck, and Mr. Leroy took an old quilt from the cab and draped it over our friend. We entered the restaurant and grabbed a seat near the front panel window where we could keep an eye on her. Others coming in for supper stopped briefly, pointing to the bulge, and then moved on expressionless. Inquiry was vastly diminished before a meal in South Alabama.

Mr. Leroy excused himself to go to the restroom, and while he was gone I made my way back to the truck. I stood in the drizzle gazing with penetrating eyes through the quilt at this little lady dressed in her wedding dress, mud clinging to every thread. Trying to make sense of her life I felt Miss Emily brush near again and whisper, "She's Nobody."

"Yes, I know."

But it was different. She had nobody. Left out on the porch to be hauled off like garbage, playing second fiddle to a football game, she was banished indeed. Standing there, I realized I might have been a Nobody, but I had somebody, a lot of somebodies on Rock Springs Road who loved me. I sensed several generations and many neighbors looking over my shoulder. I sighed heavily and went back inside.

Mr. Leroy thoroughly enjoyed his hamburgers and the home-made fries. He conversed with the waitresses as if they were his daughters. Everyone loved him and treated him like a father. Most of his weight had slipped to his belly over the years, and he looked like a volcano. When he laughed, which was often, he erupted through his smile. I, however, was not enjoying my food as much. I could not take my eyes off the matriarch outside, and the effects of the tobacco had not fully worn off. Finally he said it was time to leave. He tipped the waitress heavily, as usual, and we made our way back to the truck.

We drove her to the funeral home. They were not overly enamored with the condition, but they paid Mr. Leroy anyway. He refused it, as was his custom. An intern removed the chains and began sliding her onto a gurney to transport her through the funeral home's back door. As an afterthought, Mr. Leroy, with tobacco oozing, grabbed the young man's arm, stared him dead in the eye and said, "Be careful with the dress, she was married in it." It was said with such reverence, the boy removed his hat. That was the last we saw of her.

The ride home was quiet as I tried to comprehend what had happened. Mr. Leroy had not lied. It was an odd job, one I would never forget nor repeat. I couldn't help but wonder if we had given this little lady her first adventure beyond the hollow of her little world, her first trip to a food establishment. Maybe she felt like a Somebody for once. It was a shame we spoiled her beautiful dress on her debut with society. Mr. Leroy interrupted my thoughts.

"Did ya have fun, Gibut?"

I had only to consider it for a moment. I could have stayed at home and spent the afternoon watching football. I could have walked in the woods behind the trailer contemplating life as I used to do on the farm in the Mallard Woods back on Rock Springs

Road. I could have spent the day reading history or writing letters home. These were all enjoyable to me, but I was reminded of my youth on the farm. Life is best when you're doing it, not reading or thinking about it. To have memories tomorrow, you have to make a few today.

The rain, the mud, the stench, the dried vomit on my shirt, the spinning head, the soaked body, the feeling of death on my hands, it all added up to an obvious answer.

"Yes, sir, I had a lot of fun."

He smiled, and black ooze formed at the corners of his mouth.

CHAPTER FIFTEEN

I continued to work for Mr. Leroy, but I also picked up a part-time job with a veterinarian. If I had any thoughts of becoming a vet, those hopes were dashed when I took organic chemistry, which I discovered was a course much like a weed killer: it removed all of the undesirables. When I entered the first class, I noticed about half of the students had dark circles under their eyes, and looked haggard and withdrawn—some even twitched nervously. It looked like what I imagined those arriving at Ellis Island looked like. "Give me your tired, your poor, your huddled masses yearning to be free," as the Emma Lazarus poem says. The professor told us that half of the students in his class would fail; a slight grin formed, but he then went on to detail the course. I discovered that those nervous students were giving it a second try—masochists I assumed. I had always imagined that being a vet was pretty simple: if the animal is sick, you either sell it or give it enough penicillin to heal it or kill it. And I had no idea carbon was so important. Terrified at the prospects of failing a class, I attended all three sections, amounting to nine classes a week, only to emerge with a C. I was never so proud of being average in my life. It was obvious, though, that I would neither be a Rhodes Scholar nor a veterinarian. Having decided against becoming a vet, I resigned myself to working with one.

Dr. Thomas was a no-nonsense businessman who had his fingers in multiple enterprises around Auburn. He reminded me of Thomas Jefferson in his abilities. He never shied away from any business venture, and he expected total obedience from those surrounding him. Much like my father, he was not to be questioned, and I feared and respected him, in that order. He was the antithesis of Mr. Leroy.

He had an employee, a black man named Pet Wilson, whose survival depended on his ability to make others feel superior. He laughed at all the jokes, even when he was the subject. He knew how to appear to be the fool, but he was no fool. He had a drinking problem, a difficult home life, and no apparent dreams other than surviving day by day. He had a raspy laugh from smoking, and he always lowered his head and cut his eyes around to see if anyone was listening. Outgoing, but always guarded, he was a small man with a huge grin, and he found the humor in the simplest situations. He, his son, and I worked together feeding the hundreds of cattle

Dr. Thomas owned. When we went out to feed in his short-bed red Toyota, Pet always told me to sit in the middle of the front seat and put his son on the outer passenger side. I never understood why until I asked him one day out of curiosity.

"Pet, is there any particular reason you always stick me in the middle?"

"I was wonderin' when you were ever going to get around to asking," he said, toying with me. "You didn't know it, but we are known around town as the Oreo Crew. I have to keep your creamy white ass in the middle to keep our reputation." So we were the Oreo Crew. It wasn't exactly as noble as belonging to the Knights of the Round Table, but in South Alabama I took what distinction I could get, and soon it grew on me. There were only three of us, but community is community, and we became very close.

One morning the Oreo Crew assembled at the vet clinic to do an unusual job. We were told to buy several packages of hot dogs, bring them to the clinic, cut them up into small pieces, and infuse a small pill in each one. It made no sense, but who was I to ask questions. We had several gallons of infused hot dogs by mid-morning. We were then instructed to take them to the edge of the property and throw them out in the fencerow, but it was imperative that this be done at night. So we waited.

Dr. Thomas depended on Pet for just about everything. I had no idea the extent of his dependence until one day during a lull in the busy day at the animal clinic, he yelled at Pet to get the operating scissors. Dr. Thomas removed his coat and stretched out on the operating table. I was sweeping the floor, trying to mind my own business, wondering what surgery Pet might perform on his boss. Apparently this was a regular event, as he nonchalantly took Dr. Thomas's shoes off, removed his socks, and commenced to clean out and cut his toenails. Pet even did it with a smile.

The pedicure was cut short when an elderly lady entered the surgery. She was carrying a pet squirrel wrapped in a worn blanket. Dr. Thomas jumped up off the table, barefoot, and approached the lady with apparent concern. When he felt the cold of the floor, he grimaced, but Pet was already standing there with shoes in hand.

"What can I do to help, ma'am?" Dr. Thomas offered while slipping his shoes on.

"It's my pet squirrel; it's sick, and I don't know what to do."

"Squirrel, a pet?" His eyebrows knitted, "How old is it?"

"I've had her about five years."

Dr. Thomas pushed his glasses back on top of his head, indicating he knew what the problem was. "Just leave it with me, and I'll let you know by tomorrow how it's doing." The little lady smiled nervously, and left quietly. When the door closed behind her, Dr. Thomas took the squirrel in the back room. I heard a loud whack, and he emerged refocused. He told the receptionist to call the lady the next day and tell her the squirrel had died during the night.

"Tell her there's no charge."

Next on the agenda was the treatment of a large dog in the back run. It had been barking and growling all morning, and it was time to deal with it. One of my jobs on the weekend was to clean the pens by hosing them out. It was always satisfying to have a nice metal fence between me and the dogs.

"Come on, Gilbert. It's time for your introduction to dogs."

I was not aware that I needed an introduction. I had owned dogs all of my life. There were those I loved like my German shepherd, Boozer, and those I hated like Suzie, the chihuahua, that I sacrificed at the altar of penicillin. I had shot sick dogs and run over more than my share, but I sincerely loved them, evidenced by my housing three Irish setters in Mr. Leroy's trailer. All three of them slept with me each night, which actually improved the aroma of my humble abode.

The dog in the clinic that day had an abscess that needed to be punctured. It was too big to take to the back room and do a loud whack. Besides, sick dogs meant money. People paid exorbitant prices for the simplest cures for their pets, especially those living in the trailer parks near the clinic. They may have lacked the resources for a nice home, but they took care of their pets. Back home we just let them die if they got very sick, but here people treated these animals like family members, meaning Dr. Thomas could charge a lot.

As the two of us approached the kennel, the dog went ballistic, snarling and foaming like it was rabid. Dr. Thomas never looked at me, he just said he was going to grab the dog by the tail. When he did, he wanted me to grab it by the head. I was not excessively clever, but I knew which end of a dog had teeth. I was taught to respect authority, however, and to do what I was told. He reminded me of my father, and you don't argue with men who live on pedestals.

It went as planned. He grabbed the tail and, when the dog turned to bite him, I grabbed it behind the head, then put it between my legs and held it securely. If I had hesitated for an instant, the dog would have had an early lunch of Dr. Thomas. I have to admit, he knew what he was doing and the job was finished quickly. He packed up his tools and walked out.

"But, Dr. Thomas, how I am going to let go of this head full of teeth by myself?"

"Figure it out, but don't hurt the dog."

I heard him laughing all the way back into the clinic. I began talking nicely to the dog as I dragged him to the kennel gate. He had that vengeful tiger's eye, and my soft voice was having no effect. It was either he or I, so I mustered up all my strength and slung him against the wire fence as far as I could and hastily exited.

The remainder of the day was spent doing a regular assortment of jobs around the clinic until closing, which was about dusk. I was getting ready to leave when Pet reminded me we had one last job. I had forgotten about the hotdogs. It wasn't quite dark yet, so he said he wanted me to go to his home and teach him how to kill his hog and turn it into tasty breakfast morsels. I had told him stories about hog killing day back home, so I supposed he wanted me to look at his setup.

He lived in a well-kept, rental trailer. The lawn was primarily dirt, and there were no shrubs, trees, or flowers. The two-step porch leading to the only door was concrete with two-by-four hand railings. The lady he lived with wasn't his wife, but they had been together a long time. He loved her, though he talked about her in less-than-admiring ways. It was a strange relationship. Both of them verbally attacked each other relentlessly. They argued in front of me as if I were not even there. Then when it looked like blows were likely, they laughed, hugged, and went back to their business. They did not pretend; they got it out in the open, and it seemed to work well for them.

He took me out back, where he proudly showed me his pig; it was huge. It was some sort of a cross between a civilized hog and a wild boar. I had never seen anything quite like it. He then took me to see his scalding vat. To hog enthusiasts, the presenting of the scalding vat was equal to a man showing off his new Lamborghini. We walked up to the outside of a building. I thought we were going to enter when he commented.

"Do you think it's big enough?"

I didn't see anything, but then my eyes dropped to my feet where I spied a five gallon bucket. It wasn't big enough for the pig's head! I looked at Pet helplessly, and he burst into laughter. "Got ya, Oreo." He had lured me to his home on the pretense of giving him advice, but he really only wanted me to admire his pig. He had few possessions. So we stood there that evening, talking the finer points of his magnificent swine. When ownership is reduced to something on four legs, every aspect becomes important. He admired that pig like a man who owns a million dollar racehorse. It was dusk, and he already had gin on his breath. His eyes were bloodshot and the whites were yellow, but he had a dignity, an integrity that inspired me. I stood beside him admiring his pig in the pines of Alabama, but there was nowhere else I wanted to be. Serenity is elusive, and it picked this obscure moment to surface, reminding me what it was to be human. We just stood there in total silence, not really looking at the pig, just being friends.

It was dark by now, so we returned to the clinic. Pet retrieved the keys to the vet truck, and we picked up the bucket of doctored hotdogs. Then he drove to the destination. His plan was to drive around the border of Dr. Thomas's property while I held on to the back of the vet truck throwing the hot dogs into the fencerow as instructed. He was in a hurry as he bounced through the field, and I almost fell off several times. Finished, he drove like a madman back to the clinic. He hurriedly said good night and escaped into the evening. It all seemed very strange.

Two days later, we noticed a large number of buzzards circling the trailer park that bordered Dr. Thomas's property. I told Pet we needed to check it out. He said calmly that I needed to stay away from there for a few more days. Then he told me what we had done. The dogs from the trailer park had killed several calves, and Dr. Thomas's solution was to poison as many predators as possible. I didn't condone such actions, but I understood. Back home, our neighbors endorsed the policy that if anyone's dog attacked another's animals, it was acceptable, even expected, to kill the dog. No one would have questioned it. But here it was different; these were not farmers, and they did not grasp the importance of keeping predators confined. Some of the dogs in the trailer park were rushed to Dr. Thomas's clinic for treatment. Some survived, and he became a hero.

Dr. Thomas called me early one Saturday morning to help work some cattle. He said it wouldn't take long, so I arrived at six in the morning. Working cattle meant we ran them through a chute and did any number of jobs, from deworming to vaccinating. That day we did both, plus pregnancy checking, which involved putting his arm up the anus of the cow, giving him an opportunity to palpate downward to the uterus. Dr. Thomas wore a plastic sleeve, for obvious reasons. My job was to hold the tail out of his way so the cow could not switch it into his face. We had been at it for hours, having checked hundreds of cattle. There were only a few left when a tail slipped from my hand and slapped him across the face. He let out a string of obscenities, spitting between syllables. Then he turned on me without reservation and slapped me across the face with his manure-laden glove. It stunned me. It wasn't the sharp pain, but the humiliation. I glanced over at Pet, who wasn't surprised. He just smiled sadly. For an instant, and only an instant, I was in his shoes. He had endured this type of treatment often in his life. Dr. Thomas threw a towel at me to clean my face, but I thought the appearance of a handmade badge might make a better point. I did not retaliate, but finished the work that day with a beautifully tattooed imprint of his glove on my cheek. Then I walked home. I think I had shiitake mushrooms for supper.

As fall gave way to winter, pasture grew scarce and preparations were made for feeding the cows. Dr. Thomas mixed chopped round bales with chicken manure. It smelled awful, and I wondered why any animal ate it, except that as my uncle used to say, "It's better than a snowball." The ammonia was so strong that just the feeding of it burned my nostrils. On paper it worked nutritionally, but getting the cows to eat it was challenging, so he mixed all of this concoction in a large mixer on a truck and added molasses for flavor. It worked. I understood this because it was the way I ate. I just mixed all my vegetables together, and if I had some molasses, poured it on making a total mixed ration.

He called me on a cold winter evening to go with him to Atlanta to pick up a used feed mixing truck he had recently purchased. He never bought anything new because he never operated it. Atlanta was two hours away. I reluctantly agreed to go. I had not developed the knack of turning anyone down.

As we headed north, he talked about a variety of topics, but after a while he told me about his family. His normal crusty voice turned affectionate as he described his daughters and his wife, whom he cared for deeply. I saw a different side, a vulnerable side of this man who appeared distracted and driven. He even talked about Pet and the many ways he had tried to help him. It was hard to put it all together. The monologue continued almost to Atlanta. He said more in that trip than I had ever heard him speak of anything. He was calm, thoughtful, and sincere about the important aspects of life. At one point he grew very quiet. Suddenly, he said, "Gilbert, I need to give you some advice." I knew he was going to tell me something about the importance of family, that time is short, and I should live as if each day were my last, or some other quip shared around a campfire that would change my life.

He continued. "If you ever find yourself lost, and you stop for directions, and if the person instructing you uses his hands to point here and there, just walk away. Those people are just as lost as you are." That was it. It was the only advice he gave me in the year I worked with him. I can't say it is altogether false, so whenever someone asks me for directions, I put my hands behind my back, and smile, as I struggle to communicate.

Time tripped on quickly, and we made it to Atlanta by eleven that night. Upon arrival, we made our way to the back lot where the mixer truck was waiting for us. He told me to drive it since he didn't want me driving his nice truck. It was winter, and an uncharacteristic snow for the region was falling. Again, I agreed. He said he would lead so that I wouldn't get lost. We were in downtown Atlanta.

I was nervous about being in the middle of a metropolis, but he assured me all was well. His nature changed abruptly, and he said, "You can't get lost because all roads lead to the clinic." He broke into laughter and jumped into his warm truck. The mixer truck had no heat and the floorboard had holes in it, allowing December to flow unabated. We left as the snow was accumulating on the road. The traffic was sparse. It couldn't have been more than a minute before I lost him. He drove off and left me in downtown Atlanta. Now I was on my own. I did not have a lot of experience with road signs, we had none on Rock Springs Road. I was directionally challenged from birth, but I was never actually lost, just temporarily destination poor. I drove around Atlanta for an hour or so until I finally made my way south.

The ice and snow continued to build on the windshield, and the wipers were poor at best. Occasionally I rolled the window down and stuck my head out to see better, then back inside to thaw. On the way back to the clinic, I had a sharp conversation with him in my mind. I had developed great oratorical skills in my youth. I could really lambaste my father in a monologue. My words were razor sharp, but only in my mind. My execution of these well-thought-out speeches always fell flat. I came back to the present when I noticed Dr. Thomas's truck parked on the side of the interstate only a quarter mile ahead. It appeared that he was waiting, but as I approached, I noticed the light was on in the cab, and his head was cocked against the side window. He was asleep.

I started to honk so he would know I was passing, but something deep inside held my hand steady. There was more at stake here. I thought about that day working the cattle when I felt the sting of his palm, I thought of him leaving me in Atlanta, the loud whack of the squirrel, dead dogs, and I thought of Pet Wilson and toenails. My hand returned to my side, and a great peace covered me. The remainder of the trip was pure joy. I made it back, parked the truck under the breezeway at the clinic, and walked home.

The next weekend I returned to work at the clinic. Dr. Thomas didn't say anything at first, then he calmly asked what happened to me on my trip back from Atlanta. I said that the trip was uneventful, and I was happy to help him out. I added that I would be glad to do it all over again if I ever had the chance.

"I waited for you half the night parked out on the interstate," he said with irritation.

There was a silent, uncomfortable lull. Timing is everything, and I waited patiently for the moment.

"Why did you do that?" I finally asked, "I couldn't get lost; all roads lead to the clinic."

He looked up sharply. Then a faint smile moved across his face. He tried to hide it, but it was undeniable. There was a noticeable change in our relationship after that, a marked improvement in respect, both ways. Even so, he continued to operate his vet clinic in his own unique way: whacking, cussing, and demeaning others. There was no denying it, though; he was an excellent veterinarian and a wise businessman. But I think he missed his true calling. He would have made a great organic chemistry professor.

CHAPTER
SIXTEEN

Attending classes at Auburn and working for Mr. Leroy and Dr. Thomas left very little time for social functions. People my own age, in general, frightened me, and it never dawned on me that any of my peers would see me as a potential friend. I enjoyed the company of children and the elderly. They were more interesting. People my own age were just children gone astray. Also, any affiliation with a girl seemed totally absurd, as I didn't chew tobacco. Romance was foreign to me. I had sisters who I loved dearly, and cows, and, of course, my mother, but I had never experienced the institution inhabited by those through the ages who had discovered the fulfillment of the deep longings of man's heart. I was twenty years old. I could vote and fight wars, but I had never walked into the arena reserved only for lovers.

I first noticed her in Animal Science 101. It was a course reserved for cowboys who knew nothing about cows, but they had their Copenhagen emblems, so they had paid their dues and were allowed admission. I sat on the back row where I could daydream without a lot of interference. It was always in a back row where my best dreams occurred and my best thoughts came to me. It was similar to Mallard Woods back home, where I sat alone with my thought-friends. It was in a back row where, in my senior year in high school, I learned how to calculate the volume of a doughnut. It was in a back row where I learned not to go to sleep during a sermon, lest I was called out. And it was while sitting in the back row that I saw her for the first time.

On the first day of class, she walked in the door holding a stack of books to her chest. I thought she was the prettiest girl I had ever seen. Humility accompanied her short stride, reflecting poise and grace. That should have been of primary importance, but I was stuck on her face and attractive body. She was incredibly proportional. Light travels faster than anything in the universe, and we men are always introduced to physical stimuli before the more important aspects come to light. We also have difficulty with the abstract and fall back on the well-tested and verifiable reality of concrete facts, and the concrete fact was that this girl, whose name I learned was Ginny, was flawless.

I continued watching her for more than a year, always from a distance. I rehearsed what I would say if the opportunity presented itself, but no amount of practice pushed me to the point of actually doing anything about it. Just the thought of speaking to her brought fear, anxiety, and sweat. I moved out of the back row so I could hear her voice. The truth was I never really considered myself worthy, but it was nice peering through the looking glass. It reminded me of going fishing on Dry Fork. At certain times of the year, when the bass spawned, they wouldn't bite at the bait; they were preoccupied. So I edged as near to the bank as possible just to watch them in their beauty and splendor, with no thought of possessing them. Such was the case as I edged nearer to her each day. She was so wonderful.

In my second year at Auburn, we took an advanced nutrition class together. She approached me several times, asking questions about the finer points of calcium and phosphorus. It's hard to bridge the conversation when you start with minerals. All of the rehearsing was futile, and I only answered with facts, desperately trying to figure out a way to direct the conversation to her, or us, but it always ended in the Krebs cycle. Finally as the year drew to a close, she approached me and asked if I would join her at a get-together on Saturday afternoon with some of her friends. I said I would love to, but as I spoke, my head spun like I was dipping snuff again. Fortunately, I sensed Mr. Leroy near, and my confidence stabilized. I still broke out in a sweat and had to find a place to sit down after she left.

The day arrived. I put on my best blue jeans. I only had three pairs, so my best were the clean ones. I had many shirts, but only one was not wrinkled, so the decision was easy. I looked in the mirror before leaving. Unfortunately, nothing had changed overnight, but I did what I could and combed my hair. I slid into my grandmother's Chevrolet Biscayne and drove to the event. I pulled into the parking area and sat for some time. *What was I thinking?* I had no part in this story. These scenarios were reserved for other people. No one had ever accused me of being debonair, and everyone back home knew that personal hygiene was not my forte. I wore my undershirts until they turned yellow, then I turned them inside out to get more use before washing them. It seemed hopeless. What propels men to go forth in impossible odds is hard to understand, except that as Alexander Pope said, "hope springs eternal in the human breast," even if it's not wearing a clean shirt.

My lack of hygiene was established early on in my childhood. One summer I went to 4-H camp for a week. My mother packed my clothes and told me to change often, but when I arrived, the thought of using all of those clean clothes disturbed me. My mother worked so hard. She never had time for anything but caring for us. I decided to surprise her by keeping the suitcase closed the entire week. The image of her opening a suitcase of clean clothes, clapping her hands together in glee, and hugging me for my thoughtfulness kept me from the despair of spending a week away from home. Every day I played hard, and every night I slept in the same clothes. Five days and four nights with no showers. The deeper I went into the week, the fewer friends I had. It didn't matter; I couldn't keep my mind off of my mother's reaction.

I returned home Friday afternoon, walked in, plopped my suitcase down at her feet, and gave her a hug. She knew something was up. I grabbed the suitcase and her hand and led her to the living room where I laid it on the couch and opened it. I had been anticipating this moment all week. Her expression was unlike any I imagined. She stood silent, completely overcome with emotion I was sure. My mother always had the right word for every occasion, but this act of love silenced her. Then I noticed her nose twitched as she slowly turned my way. She never said a word, but she held my face in her hands and smiled. Then she whisked me off to the shower.

Now ten years later, having had a shower, I approached the knoll where a large group of students were gathered. They were doing what students do: throwing Frisbees, strumming guitars, lying on blankets in shorts talking to girls doing the same. Then I saw her, and she was walking toward me. Knots formed in my gut, but the die was cast. We met in the open field, and she seemed pleased to see me. We walked together to the epicenter of the party where she introduced me to a number of friends, including her boyfriend. I smiled, shook his hand, and died.

The remainder of the afternoon I spent observing them from a distance. It was like watching a sad rerun, knowing I was powerless to change the outcome. Finally, we all gathered in a circle to sing a few songs. He pulled out his guitar and began singing. I'll have to admit he was handsome, and he more closely paralleled Ginny's beauty. As he sang, I appraised him from head to toe. He could sing, his teeth were straight with no chips, his hair was styled, his eyes danced, and his attire was perfect. I was quite sure his tee shirt wasn't inside out. With each appraisal, I felt my value diminish. It was clear I needed to go home, back to the farm to live my solitary life.

Eventually, and surprisingly, Ginny came over and introduced to me a friend who said he needed to talk to me. *What else was I to do?*

"Sure," I said, and he led me to a picnic table, away from her.

He pulled out his Bible and started telling me about salvation and the abundant life. I guess I should have been more interested in the eternal condition of my soul, but my present condition negated any other concerns. He told me how Jesus came to this earth and was betrayed by everyone, including his friends. It sounded strangely familiar. It reminded me that Jesus was also single. This did little to mend a damaged heart. He showed me a picture of two cliffs with a chasm between. He said I couldn't get to God except by crossing over by way of the cross. He talked slowly to let the words sink in, but I was numb. I couldn't get my eyes off the chasm growing between Ginny and me. I struggled just to hear what he was saying. I was raised in church, and while I had no claim to know this Christ, I think He would have noticed I was distraught and would have asked me how I was doing. He would have wanted to know why I was in such despair. I don't think he would have drawn me pictures. But He was a different sort.

Then this young man asked me if I wanted to pray the sinner's prayer. *The what?* I couldn't make the connection. To appease him I agreed, but my mind was miles away. So I smiled and prayed, and when I raised my bowed head, he was crying. So was I, but for a different reason. He gave me a hug and walked away. The sun dropped lower and dusk settled in. I wanted to say goodbye to Ginny, but I just left. It was springtime. I went home and gathered all of my dirty clothes together. I washed everything. I don't know why, it just seemed right. I couldn't do much about the soiled soul, but I had to start somewhere.

I saw her occasionally in other classes, and we took a few field trips together. The pressure was off now, and I just enjoyed her friendship. I still didn't know much about girls, but I was beginning to know a lot about Ginny, and I thoroughly enjoyed the knowledge. The last week before leaving Auburn, she invited me to go with some friends to Hotel Tallassee, a little diner popular with college eaters. I considered what to wear, but the jig was up, and I realized that silk purses don't come from sows' ears. I wore an old Columbo trench coat and my shiny plastic shoes that were usually reserved for Sunday. These represented the most notable of my attire. I brushed my teeth. It was a great time. I was only a spectator, and she was still as pretty as ever, and her voice had become a song I heard often. There wasn't much I didn't like about her, and while she was not within my grasp, I still enjoyed her presence.

I finished my two years at Auburn in the spring. My mother drove three hundred miles to help me pack up and return home. As I loaded the Chevrolet Biscayne, a strange sensation enveloped me. I was going back to my farm on Rock Springs Road, but as we drove home I felt I was going in the wrong direction. Just two years before, when I left the farm, I remembered thinking I'd turn around and go home at each interstate exit. Now, I felt the same way, going in the opposite direction. I couldn't get her out of my mind, and the further I drove the more homesick I became. It dawned on me that home was not a place.

That summer a conflict arose. I couldn't keep my mind off of this girl and how much I felt like I loved her. I knew I couldn't really love her because I didn't know her well enough for that. You can fall in a hole, but you can't fall in love. Infatuation is spontaneous, like winning an apple pie at a state fair raffle, but love is taking the time to buy the ingredients, mix them, put them in a pan, and bake them at 350 degrees for an hour. That apple pie just tastes better. But as much as I was sensing a love for her, I was also discovering how little I loved myself, and I couldn't figure out why.

I was raised in a cause-and-effect home. If this, then that. Deductive reasoning always led to logical conclusions. Everything I received was compensation for something I had done. Nothing was free. I had always attended church, and my goal in life was to be good enough or do enough good things to pass the test and end up in heaven. At death, the ancient Egyptians had their hearts placed on a scale balanced against the feather of truth by Anubis, the jackal-headed god. If their life was not virtuous enough, the Devourer swallowed them. Because it was impossible for me to know how many good things were required to be virtuous, I knew I would have to wait until death to find out how the scale tilted and what waited for me behind door number three. The conversation with that young man from Auburn about chasms and Jesus kept haunting me. He indicated that there was a way to God, but I couldn't remember him saying anything about good deeds. So I started reading my Bible and other books.

As it turned out, I found evidence that it is difficult to determine absolute truth. Many Christians have strong opinions about a variety of doctrinal issues, many of which do not matter. The more I read, the more questions I asked, and the more convinced I was that we were like the seven blind men who tried to describe an elephant while holding on to different parts of its body. All accounts were accurate, just not complete. One thing was for sure, I could not be good enough to earn anything good. I realized even my best efforts were self-serving. If everything I did was to get something for myself, then it was selfish and could hardly be love. I felt the chasm growing wider and wider, and I was sure I could not leap it in a single bound. I was stuck.

Then one evening I went out to the silage trough to feed the cows. I sat on top of the covered augur, and while the sweet smelling corn silage poured down the trough, I knew I could never live a life of virtue and goodness. The rootstock was damaged and could never produce anything virtuous. I prayed to God, telling Him that I needed help because, simply put, I was helpless. I had read that Jesus came here to take the sins of everyone and die once and for all. I had heard this my whole life. It just never dawned on me that everyone included me. So I asked Him to do for me what I could not, and I think that is what people call salvation.

Now something interesting happened. Nothing. There were no signs in the heavens, no shooting stars. I felt no different, except a slight lifting of a heavy burden. I had read of people's conversions, and how they were always accompanied by spectacular events. There were stories about people who had done horrible things, and then presto-change-o, all was right. That did not happen to me. I finished feeding the cows, went home, told no one, and went to bed.

The practical and most wonderful part about it all was that previously I had attempted to earn my way to heaven by doings things for the sole purpose of acquiring something. Now everything was turned on its head. I had Christ, salvation, and heaven already. Now everything I did was not motivated for my own benefit, it was simply a way of saying thank you to Someone who had given me door number three. I concluded that everything I did that was motivated to make me look good was a failure, no matter what it might look like to everyone else, and everything I did that honored Christ or others was a success no matter how much of a failure it appeared to be to the world. Now, for the first time, I could concentrate on others, not myself.

But I also learned that in many ways I had not changed. I still had bitter thoughts and wrong motivations. I may have been in the presence of Christ in heaven, theoretically, but down here on earth I was still a mess. The difference was that I had Someone working on me. It would take a lifetime, but at least progress, two steps forward, one step back, was inevitable. I was not a rags-to-riches story. I was not a drug abuser turned saint overnight. I was not a Christian athlete who has a biography written about him because he was a winner. I just asked God to save me while I sat in a silage trough surrounded by, appropriately, manure. I believed He did, and that was enough.

I transferred to the University of Tennessee in Knoxville that fall to complete my degree and be near my three sisters. I lived with my two best friends in a trailer that we questionably called a home. It was there that I wrote Ginny the letter, revealing my feelings for her. It seemed hopeless, but so did salvation until I learned the truth. Never say die, there are no lost causes, I had heard my mother say. A week later Ginny called late one night. Ben answered the phone, and he smiled knowingly when he handed me the receiver. I braced myself for the obvious. What a fool I was to consider such an outrageous proposition. I heard her voice, and it was as sweet as ever. She proceeded to tell me that she had broken up with her boyfriend, and how sad she was because of it. Actually, he had broken it off with her. We both silently cried. She said she wasn't interested in any relationship now, she needed time to heal. That was enough for me.

There have truly only been two big decisions in my life. One was what to do with this man who, two thousand years ago, claimed to be God. This would affect my eternal world. Jesus had killed religion in my life once and for all. He showed me that love was more than a scale. The other decision was what to do with this girl who I claimed was the most extraordinary person in this world. She would affect my present. For the first time, I felt something I could not define. Love laughs at deductive reasoning. In less than six months, I had encountered the despair of not being able to love myself. Then I found the Remedy. I had also found someone with skin on who brought the idea of romantic love to a tangible reality. That's a lot to take in.

My universe was expanding at light speed, and the mystery of the unknown created in me a sense of fascination and intrigue. Possibilities were boundless, but with this emotional upheaval came strange vibrations of despair and depression that could have elevated me to new heights of anxiety, except that I had living examples of those who were forever near. Mr. Leroy would have smiled and let the snuff ooze, Pet Wilson would have reminded me I was a member of the prestigious Oreo Crew, and my mother would have held my face in her hands and smiled. I had nothing to fear.

CHAPTER
SEVENTEEN

After graduating from college, I spent the year working with my father. Having done this successfully after high school, I looked forward to repeating the experience. A college education, or at least a piece of paper stating certain requirements were met, can be deceptive to a young man. I was 24, and, of course, I knew more than my father. That year turned into the most difficult one of my life. He and I saw nothing eye to eye; we argued about everything. The fault did not lie with either of us. We were both strong-willed individuals who strove for acceptance within ourselves. No amount of success would have given my father any degree of peace, and I had accomplished nothing noteworthy, so I was vying to find my own meaning as well.

I also began finding my voice in speaking up for my mother. My father had a very demanding and overbearing mother, and I often wondered when he married if his goal was to put his mother in her place, using his wife as a substitute. His attitude toward her created a major stumbling block in our relationship. I have heard it said if a man wants to have the heart and respect of his children, he must first love their mother. In this he was neglectful, and there was nothing he could do in the way of love for me to close the gap.

One day during lunch I was sitting at the dinner table talking with him. Momma was washing the dishes at the sink when he made a very demeaning remark to some question she asked. Daddy had a college degree, and Momma did not, but it was evident who was more educated. Momma read a lot, memorized poetry, and was generally interested in everything. He felt threatened by her intelligence, so when he saw an opportunity to take her down a notch, he took it. I had listened to this for years, stuffing it down deep inside each time. For some reason, on this day it put me over the top. I stood up and looked him eye to eye, always difficult, and yelled, "You think you know so much!" That was it. I had waited so long to deliver my monologue, had practiced it endless times, waxed eloquently to my dogs, but when it came time for my soliloquy that was all that came out.

I stormed out of the kitchen, down a short flight of stairs leading outside, but as I turned to exit, a powerful force exploded on my right eye. I hit the floor, unconscious. I woke up a few minutes later and figured out what had happened. I can't remember the pain, but I can still hear the crack of his knuckles against my eye socket. A lot goes through your mind when you're lying on your back, having been put there by someone you love, admire, and respect. My father was not a hard man. He was passionate and demanded no more of others than he did of himself. His integrity was as firm as his tightly set jaw. I had seen him stand against wrong on many occasions. He was honest and played no favorites. I really considered him King Arthur, and although his treatment of my mother lacked chivalry, I enjoyed being a part of his Round Table.

But he had a temper. In high school his nickname was Flash Gordon because of his speed on the basketball court, but the flash we knew resembled an electrical impulse that came out of nowhere like lightning, scorching everything around him. His anger was a force not to be reckoned with. On the other hand, my father was real; he was not milk toast, and I was far happier being his son than to have been the son of a father who taught his children they were the center of the universe. Fear is not all bad, and his aura kept me on the straight and narrow most of my youth.

I picked myself up off the floor. I didn't regard my dignity as compromised; I was a Gordon, and we could pull ourselves up by our bootstraps. But, with blurred vision, finding my bootstraps was the immediate problem at hand. I only had one objective as I put my cap back on and headed out to find him. He had not gone far, only to the gate leading out of the yard. He was staring out toward the barn. As I approached him, he squared up to receive whatever was coming, he knew not what. Neither did I. There was sadness in his demeanor, the fire spent. I walked up, toe to toe, and stood, reflected in his eyes. I could tell he was trying to avoid looking at my swollen eye. Standing there in the silence, we gazed at each other in various forms of pain. And then I spoke.

"Daddy, I am sorry for what I said, I didn't mean it."

Again, I don't know where those words came from, but they obviously represented my better angel, while my darker side seethed. I could see he wanted to say something, but he nodded and walked away, head down. We never talked about it.

I do not tell this to criticize my father, but to accentuate the point that families love each other in ways that may seem harsh to others. My father gave a whole new meaning to the phrase *being grounded*. I hear this today in reference to children being restricted to only six hours on the computer instead of ten. I'll take the black eye any time. To this day, there is no ill feeling about the whole incident. I regard it as building character, and I am thankful to have been the son of a fiery personality. My father was an intense man who taught me the more important aspects of life, generally without words. He taught me by observation, which is better than words. The only residual effect of this encounter on me is that when I am confronted, and I feel my anger growing, I slip my hands into my pockets for safe keeping.

That summer he took my mother on a trip to Mexico for several weeks to see her sister. They never went anywhere, so this was a special occasion. It had been a very dry summer and silage-chopping season was only a couple of weeks away. He said they would return in time. He had always been in charge, and it is hard to give up that control, especially if you are good at what you do. When my father met me for the first time, I was a newborn. That being his first impression, it could not be altered. I was always a child to him. So he hoped to return soon because he wasn't sure this infant could carry on without him. Everything seemed to be in order as they departed. What neither he nor any of us realized was that as they were headed south to visit the land of the Aztecs, whose land was ravaged by the Spaniards, the armyworm was headed north toward Gordon's Villa to ravage our farm.

Armyworms resemble in destruction what locusts have done down through the centuries. Because of their complete destruction of food crops, they were considered plagues just as real as viruses. We weren't worried about dying, but we knew they could strip an entire field of crops in days. I noticed the corn showing unusual signs of stress, so when I investigated, I discovered millions of armyworms waging war on the corn. It was only five feet tall, and I knew it would be gone in less than a week. We had to act quickly, and it was impossible to call Daddy for advice since he was in Mexico.

We chopped the corn silage in its green stage, making it so wet it might ruin in the silo. Silage has to be put up at the right moisture or it will sour. Good fermentation requires a certain amount of oxygen to initiate the production of the good bacteria. Too much moisture eliminates the oxygen and encourages the bad bacteria, which results in sour silage with an ammonia type smell, and the cows will not eat it. To counter the excessive water of the premature corn plant we were blowing into the silo, we needed to add some dry matter.

I ordered many loads of bagged, crushed corn from the co-op to mix with it. The math may have been rudimentary, but farming was not an exact science, and we were comfortable with estimations. We dumped the corn on each load of silage, one bag at a time. It was extremely laborious and time consuming, but our backs were against the wall. All week, running dawn to dark, and we finally finished. Near the end, the worms had nearly completely destroyed the little that remained, but we finished. It would take several weeks to see if the gamble paid off.

Daddy and Momma returned. I was confident in my decision, but still he held the scepter, and I never wanted to disappoint him. When I sat down and explained what had happened and how we had handled the dilemma, he sat quietly for a few moments. I waited for some movement of affirmation. He simply nodded. His deep blue eyes exercised an uncharacteristic calm I could not read. We were sitting around the same green kitchen table where I had spoken disrespectfully to him months before. No one was there, just the two us. Then he said, "It just might work." Those words meant more than any pat on the back. It was comparable to "You brilliant boy, you are amazing." I showed him how we did it, and I sensed he was very proud of what we had attempted. He nodded over and over and reiterated, "It just might work." There was something so wonderful about his face that day, and it is that face I will never forget.

Miraculously, my relationship with Ginny had sprouted and grown quickly that summer. We dated that fall with plans to marry the following spring. I had written her parents, who were in Africa, asking for their daughter's hand in marriage. It is said that distance makes the heart grow fonder, so 5000 miles was sufficient in receiving an affirmative answer. They thought much higher of me than they should have. Ginny came from a prominent family in Nashville who were influential in the signing of the Cumberland

Compact that established Nashville. My family was outside the fort doing the dirty work. Now her parents signed the papers on our relationship, and I was invited inside. Our dating was simple, I drove sixty miles to her farm on one weekend to help work her beef cows. Then she traveled sixty miles to our farm on the next weekend and milked cows. This long-distance relationship kept us out of a lot of trouble.

Her parents raised more than beef cattle. They also cultivated people, founding a commune for anyone who wanted to come and be a part of a Christian community. Within only a few years, they attracted people ranging from those from Harvard College to those trying to avoid motorcycle gangs. Some were just everyday people trying to sort out this thing called life. Others came to work on the farm and help restore the old farmhouse the family had moved into. On Friday nights, everyone gathered on the front porch for a meal and to sing together. The food was orchestrated primarily by Ginny's mom, whose cuisine was different from what I knew. I was raised on meat and potatoes with plenty of fat, grease, and butter. Ginny's mother supported the idea that vegetables and herbs were better for you, and she always mixed a variety of foods that were never intended to exist together. Regardless of my opinions, I learned that everyone had a different take on life, and if I listened, I might just learn something.

One Saturday afternoon I was painting the exterior wood siding of the old farmhouse with two other fellows I had never met. As I stroked, I listened to their conversation. They were discussing the finer points of dating, so I thought I should pay attention for possible hints. They were both Vanderbilt students, so I assumed they were rich in intelligence. One asked the other what he was looking for in a relationship. I think he meant what type of girl turned him on. After some thought, as is the custom of a wise man, he answered, "The ultimate goal of dating is to receive spiritual growth and encouragement." I almost fell off the ladder.

There were many aspects that attracted me to Ginny: her love of life, her honesty, her faithfulness to friends, her sincerity, her compassion for others, and I loved her voice. I could sit and listen to her forever. But she was also beautiful, and I thoroughly enjoyed, not spiritual growth and encouragement, but physical hugs and kisses. Holding her in my arms was mesmerizing and, as the only girl I ever kissed, she was the best. I was thankful I didn't attend Vanderbilt; they were not much fun.

Having received her parents' consent on our marriage, I prepared for the occasion of proposal. Early in the week, I sent her a box of what looked like a dozen roses, but when she opened it, a dozen peacock feathers awaited her. I always equated the peacock with the Greek god Argus who was the hundred-eyed protector of Io, a beautiful girl changed into a white heifer. Ginny's father raised white Charolaise cattle, so it all seemed fitting. Peacock feathers were also longer-lasting than common roses. She needed to know exactly what lay in store for her in the next fifty years if she agreed to this precarious arrangement.

I arrived that day at her farm on Beech Creek about the middle of the day after lunch. We walked up the long lane leading to her favorite thinking stump at a clearing on Old Colorado. We were accompanied by her old sheep dog, Joe-Joe Amote Pootie Face. In Latin, his name was loosely translated as Joe-Joe I love your Poot

Face. He spent most of his days rubbing his face in dead carcasses, hence the name. He was ancient, and we took our time so that he could keep up. Special occasions become lasting memories with the presence of those sages embodied in our pets.

We finally reached our destination, and I invited Ginny to take a seat on the stump. Joe- Joe sat between us as guardian. He was not convinced of my intentions yet. I sang my asking. As I began to sing, I had a flashback to that miserable picnic at Auburn when my adversary triumphed over me. My teeth were not straight, I couldn't carry a tune in a bucket, the lyrics were sincere but not poetic, and my voice annoyed Joe-Joe. He kept twisting his head like he had an ear infection. To my credit, I had a clean tee shirt on. It was the ultimate test for Ginny. I had nothing to offer her but a promise. I presented her the ring that had belonged to her great-grandmother. She accepted it and me. As if rehearsed, Joe-Joe Amote Pooty Face moved aside, giving his approval. Ginny and I embraced.

We married on the anniversary of when I sent the famous letter, which was also the anniversary of her parents' wedding. The year had been a struggle as I tried to find myself apart from my family. The struggle was so intense that it convinced me to take my bride elsewhere to establish our autonomy. Ginny was home to me now, and place was not as significant. We packed up our belongings as we prepared to move. I did not know that the next year my father would be diagnosed with Parkinson's Disease at the age of sixty-two. The face I saw the day we left would not be the same face I saw three short years later when we returned. He would not be the same man. But we didn't know that. We were newly married and totally absorbed in each other, embarking on a new adventure, leaving the old behind to start our new life together on a dairy farm in upstate New York.

CHAPTER EIGHTEEN

Ginny and I moved away from home to gain distance from our families and lessen any distance they might bring to our relationship. Everyone needs time and space to establish the oneness of a marriage, so we applied for a manager's position caring for dairy cattle. We received interest from all over the country, including one from a man in Illinois who said if we would change our name to Adams, he would give us his farm and his luggage company in Chicago. I was too proud of my name to consider it. Pride always leads to regret.

We had interest from a dozen or so farms, but we finally narrowed it down to a small farm in a picturesque village in upstate New York owned by a wealthy businessman who lived primarily in Texas. Mr. Johns flew to Nashville to interview us. He wined and dined us, and we had a conversation about expectations and salary. I did not know what to ask. I just wanted to take my bride to a new home and get on with life. It was an exciting time. We agreed that night and shook on the arrangement. We would start in June.

We packed up our belongings and moved north of the Mason-Dixon Line. We knew we had totally left Dixie when we stopped at a diner in Pennsylvania, ordered sweet tea, and were given a cup of hot water, a teabag, and a glass of ice. It would take some getting used to, but we were young and nothing seemed too great an obstacle. At least they spoke English, sort of.

Raised in the South, I was suspicious of anything other than the South. No matter what anyone might say today, there are differences. Long hot days send us to the front porch more often, where we tell stories. My mother said the demise of civilization, as we know it, will occur when homes are built without front porches. This is where conversations build families and society. Heat slows down the metabolism in the South, and we talk more slowly and take longer getting to the point, if there is one. And when the conversation ends and a Southerner finally says goodbye, he doesn't really mean it. He is just saying it is time to switch topics or move to a different location, like from the sofa to the chair.

Also, Northerners drive better than we do in inclement weather. In the South inclement weather is a 10 percent forecast of snow flurries. We shut down everything except the tattoo parlors.

Then we ransack the grocery stores, go home, pull down the shades, huddle around the breakfast table to pray for deliverance, and prepare for a 24 hour siege. In the North, when they actually get three feet of snow, they roll up their sleeves, whistle a tune and drive off down the road like they're heading for the beach.

We also like our traditions and history; it is a smugness of pseudo independence. There was the American Revolution, whatever that accomplished, but then there was the American Civil War. In grammar school, we spent a whole week studying the founding of our country. Then we spent the rest of the year in the middle of the nineteenth century. No respectable Southerner would change the results of that Conflict, but that war was fought in our backyards, and we still find relics on a regular basis. We can't escape it if we try.

But I learned from our newfound friends that the American Revolution, the northern rebellion, was in their backyards, and they had a knowledge and appreciation for that Conflict that I was ignorant of. I soon fell in love with a history of our country I had passed over. It dawned on me that, as Americans, we were all just a bunch of rebels.

We became the center of attention immediately. I don't think anyone had seen a United Moving Van in that part of the country in decades. Everyone, young and old, treated us with warm interest. Then, for no apparent reason, people showed up at our door bearing gifts and desiring a conversation. This was not what I expected from people I had been told were solemn and suspicious. They were still guarded in their opinions and ideas, but they were amazingly interested in who we were and what we were doing. I was in the middle of a sentence when one visitor looked at the other and a slight smile appeared. For some reason, I felt like I was entertaining them. Walking down the street, we encountered men and women who stopped and listened intently to us. I asked them questions, trying to get to know them better, but they revealed little and returned the conversation to my court. This went on for several weeks.

Finally one evening we were talking to a pair of sisters we had grown fond of. At one point I said, "Would y'all like to have some ice cream with us?"

One of the sisters replied, "I'm sorry, what did you say?"

"Would y'all like some ice cream?" I repeated.

"Who?"

"Y'all!" I was getting annoyed.

They both grinned. Composure gave way, and they burst into laughter.

"Gilbert, I am so sorry, we do not mean to appear rude, but your … your words, your … accent." She hesitated, "We've never heard anything quite like it. We love it. You two are the rage of the town."

We did not have that deep Southern accent associated with *Gone with the Wind*. Ours was much more country, a cross between East Tennessee Appalachian and a southern Memphis drawl found in Mississippi. We were stuck in the middle and our voices reflected the cohabitation. Years later when Ginny and I took a trip to France, we visited an abandoned monastery. In place of the monks' quarters were shops with various goods for sale. One vendor was a leather maker. We entered, and as soon as I opened my mouth, the artisan froze as if he had encountered an out-of-body experience. When he could finally speak, he said the last time he had heard that accent was fifty years before when he visited Kentucky. He said it was the most beautiful dialect he had ever heard. I was standing in a shop in France where the people spoke one of the most pleasing languages in human history when this well-meaning gentleman flattered me. It worked; I bought a beautiful leather-bound journal. It was the first and last time anyone ever complimented me on my native voice. It was just country, and maybe that was what our northern friends heard when they visited us. I occasionally wondered if I would lose my accent while in New York, but a recently acquired friend assured me no amount of time could ever make a dent in an accent like mine. I couldn't tell if it was a compliment, so I smiled. He reciprocated.

As it turned out, these Northerners were the most genuine people we had ever met. They were reserved and it took time to get to know them, but once we were accepted, it felt like family. They were more honest than we were in the South. We smile and pat you on the back while we think horrid thoughts. They tell it like it is with no pretense. Eventually they invited us to many of their social gatherings for more reason than our voices, and we discovered that the Mason-Dixon myth was only that. It was true that they didn't exactly know what to do with a chicken leg to make it crispy, but they could take a worthless piece of rhubarb and perform a miracle, producing the most lip-smacking strawberry-rhubarb pie imaginable.

We did not have a day off the first year of our marriage, so we had to come up with alternative means of entertainment. We did everything we could with the limited time available. One of our favorite Saturday night activities was the weekly rat kill, which was always carried out in the presence of our new friends, who were recently engaged. They came over after supper at dark. We quietly snuck into the barn. When we were safely inside, her job was to turn the lights on and scream, which she did naturally at the sight of vermin. The remaining three of us ran through the barn knocking rats off the pipelines and killing them with shovels. It reminded me so much of home except this time there was a community at work, which is always more satisfying.

The rats were so bad that we told Mr. Johns we needed to do something about it. He said they had never been a problem before, but he would check it out. He was in his eighties, and by that time in his life details had lost their significance. The next day when he arrived, we took him to the feed bin where the infestation was complete. We opened the bin and hordes of rats ran in all directions, including some running over his shoulders and across his hat. When they quickly disappeared, he said, "Where are the rats? Gilbert, I don't have time for this." Rats were never discussed again, but we continued the Saturday night raids for entertainment.

The next day he called me into a small house on the farm property. It had been his office in earlier days and was now storage for endless piles of paperwork. He seemed jittery. He asked me to sit down on the couch. He nervously paced up and down, making me a bit uneasy myself. Then he stood before me and stared for what seemed an eternity. He was a thoughtful man, and his words were carefully chosen. He had the enviable ability to edit as he spoke.

"I have a job for you. As you know, I have made a fortune in the trucking business. I need to get rid of a lot of documents that are just out of date. You know what I mean?"

I did not know what he meant about the fortune part, but I could imagine that clutter could build up over such a long career. "Yes, sir. We all need to air out every once and a while." I smiled.

He didn't.

"I need you to take all of these boxes to the concrete trench silo and burn each piece of paper in each box, one by one, until they are all gone. Do you understand?"

"Yes, sir."

Then he got real close to my face until I could see every wrinkle, every anxiety. "Do not, under any circumstance, read any of it. Do not even glance at the headings or anything else. Do you understand?"

"Yes, sir."

It was at this point that my anxiety began to build, and I swallowed hard. I suddenly remembered him telling me stories of the trucking business. How he had started with one truck working twenty hours a day, six days a week, building a trucking empire that eventually sold for millions to a major national company. He told me stories of his countless associates, but one particular name surfaced often at strange times: Jimmy Hoffa.

Now my imagination soared. I did not keep up with national news much, but I knew Jimmy Hoffa had been declared dead in

July of 1982, and this was August of the same year. His body had never been found. I burned the contents without snooping, as he requested, but for weeks I pretended to find information leading to his grave. Perhaps in the back part of the farm where the alfalfa grew, a shallow grave waited to be discovered. Imagination is a great equalizer; it cushions the realities of regularities and changes common receipts into damning evidence and makes the burning of trash a tragic world event. Imagination is everything.

It was satisfying that he had trusted me to do the job. I grew to enjoy this eccentric man. He and his wife were very kind and patient with us. Although serious in nature, he had a genuine laugh in spite of being driven to succeed. He tried to help a fledgling couple, and on several occasions arranged for us to experience a bit of New York that we, otherwise, would have missed. One of those was a trip to New York City, where we encountered a shocking dichotomy.

We arrived at Madison Square Garden in the evening. We were told to dress in our best attire since everyone would be in tuxedos and evening gowns. I decided to wear a belt. Ginny looked glamorous whether she walked down a row of tomatoes or found herself on a fashion runway, so it didn't matter what she wore, but that night she was decked out in a way that elevated my blood pressure. We entered the huge auditorium and sat near the top to witness, of all things, a cattle sale.

This sale transported us to something imaginary. We sat in disbelief as cow after cow sold for hundreds of thousands of dollars to investors seeking ways to compensate for their huge profits. It was a tax write-off. The final animal that night was a young bull that brought a million dollars. It was purchased, we were told, by a well-known actor. My father used to say that he could swap a two-million-dollar cat for two one-million-dollar dogs. It wasn't about value, but relative investment.

Having experienced enough of Vanity Fair, we quickly exited the auditorium, descended two flights of stairs, and walked along a corridor leading outside. Just as we were leaving, I saw a cold, darkened hallway. Ginny and I stopped and stared. Lined up against the wall were five old ladies with sock hats pulled down upon their heads. Simultaneously they raised their heads and stared at us. They wore sad, kind, wrinkled faces with hollow eyes. Our dismay gave way when we noticed none of them wore socks. It was near freezing in that basement. I had never seen this side of humanity. We drove home that night in complete silence. Arriving home after midnight, we undressed for bed, and I noticed sadly that I was still wearing my socks.

We lived in a small Norman Rockwell-type village. The one-lane street bordered by beautiful New England homes was reminiscent of a simpler day. Ginny and I were raised on wide-open farms with the nearest town miles away, so we enjoyed walking this quaint street that comprised the entire town. But occasionally, just to be adventurous, we embarked on long trips to keep us from getting bored. So one Sunday morning we decided to take an odyssey to the neighboring town for church, two miles away.

The parking lot was sparse, indicating we would have little trouble finding a seat. Entering the sanctuary, we were greeted at the door by a rather tall, striking woman with a kind, intense gaze. I looked past her to a near empty auditorium. I could not put my finger on it, but something was missing. It then dawned on me the congregation was almost entirely women and children. *Where were the men?* I wondered. My eyes were drawn back to hers as she greeted us. We exchanged the expected pleasantries. Then, without warning, she asked if I would be interested in teaching a class of middle school boys. It took me by surprise and immediately my mind went back to my youth.

Although not heavily schooled, my parents were educated. Their lack of an advanced formal degree, though, motivated them to want for us what they were unable to achieve. So going to college was not negotiable. My father never suggested any particular profession, but two were forbidden. He loathed the idea of any of his children becoming a pastor or a teacher. On more than one occasion he said, "Well, if you can't do anything else, I suppose you can always teach or preach." I also often heard him say, "Those who can, do, and those who can't, teach." When I was a junior in high school, I took a test indicating what professions I had a talent for. I scored very high in math, engineering, and agriculture, but far at the bottom, almost off the chart in the zone that specified the profession I would never practice was middle school teacher. It confirmed what my father had instilled.

Looking at this tall lady who asked the forbidden, I had to give an appropriate answer. If I could use ambiguous language, I could satisfy my own conscience while putting her off. Unfortunately, I had picked up a little Christianese in my short time as a believer. Clichés are handy when you don't want to say anything but must appear sincere, so I used my old standby comment whenever I didn't have the courage to say no. "I'll pray about it."

I stood toe to toe with her. I had moved quickly and effectively, and with skill I had outmaneuvered her. I was proud of my victory until she handed me a stack of booklets and said, "While you're praying, prepare for next week. There will be a dozen boys. Most of them don't have fathers." She turned to walk away, stopped, turned back around with a smile, and said, "Good luck." She apparently had dealt with clichés and masculine fakes before.

The next week I entered a classroom of rough-looking young boys. I introduced myself and there was silence, total silence. I had prepared a lesson from the books given to me, but I had a flash of intuition that the boys weren't interested in flannel boards and stickers. I put them aside and asked if they would tell me who they were. More silence. Finally, one of them started talking about his family. One after another, the boys chimed in with tale after tale of broken homes, alcohol, divorce, and everything else. It was as if each was trying to one-up the other. I sat, stupefied at hearing their sad stories.

"My daddy's in jail. He's been there before. Momma hopes he never gets out."

"I haven't seen my dad in a long time, but he promised he would be back ... two years ago."

This went on for an hour until the Sunday school bell rang, and we all went to the main service. I didn't hear a word preached that day. I was drawn to these boys in a way I had not expected.

Week after week, we grew closer as I tried different ways to befriend them. I looked forward to seeing them, as they were fast becoming my friends. Little by little, I tried to find ways to teach them about the love of God, giving them a new idea of fatherhood.

When I hear the word father as it pertains to God, I immediately feel the weight of my relationship to my father. When I mentioned God the Father to the boys, they heard God the Drunk, God the Abuser, God the Abandoner. There was little in the term that drew them. Most of my efforts that year were failures, except that they knew I cared, and I learned that was all that really mattered. They needed someone with skin, and that was all I had to offer.

I would like to say that, after a year, the boys overcame some of their obstacles, but on the last day we sat around the same table in the same total silence we started with months before. They knew I was leaving, another man abandoning them, and I didn't have the words to help them understand. They told me more about the saga of what transpired in their lives. Nothing had really changed. I shook hands with each one, even the one I had picked up by the hair earlier in the year. He and I were closest. I don't think it was because I stretched his neck, but probably because I told him I was sorry, something new to him. I left the church that Sunday and never saw any of the boys again.

Three years before, we trespassed onto northern soil. Now preparing to leave, we knew we had been conquered by the love of a battalion of friends: a friend who made the most beautiful cradle for our new daughter, a friend who came to our home often early in the morning to pray before catching a train to New York City where he worked on Wall Street, a couple of boys who showed up on our back porch one evening with a bucket of frogs that Ginny converted into a mess of fried frog legs for supper, friends who kidnapped us one evening and took us to Tanglewood where we sat on the lawn with candelabras and listened to John Williams and the Boston Pops, an entire teenage Bible study group who gave up their Monday night time together to help us get hay in the barn right before a rain, an elderly couple barely able to get by who invited us for a meal fit for a king and queen, and on and on and on. They had become our family. It was a magical time, and they still enchant us in our thoughts and memories.

We were expecting our first child, and we decided to remain in New York until her birth, which provided for us a strange predicament. It meant her being born in the north, which just three years before would have been unthinkable. But, of course, by now all of that had changed. We had divorced ourselves from Southern pride with all of its trappings. We laughed at the absurdity of paying any attention to sectional differences, especially as it related to our voices. Besides, we had not lost our accents.

Hannah finally came, and we prepared to return home. We did our best to keep our daughter's hood tied tightly so that she wouldn't hear too many strange northern sounds that might cause her permanent damage at such an early age. One can never be too careful. Then we packed up everything ten days after her birth, said goodbye to our dear friends in this beautiful country, drove south, crossed the Mason-Dixon Line, stopped at a roadside diner, ordered iced tea … and got it.

CHAPTER NINETEEN

Returning home from New York brought us back to family and to certain spiritual events generally regarded as Southern. At certain times, usually in the spring, several congregations from nearby vicinities joined together to have a bona fide foot-washing service, which was a time of reflection and humility. Jesus set the example when he washed the disciples' feet at the last supper. Afterward, in keeping with tradition, a meal was served on the grounds, consummating the day. It was to this occasion that we were invited by Elizabeth Crump, whom we affectionately called Libs. She had worked for Ginny's mother as a house cleaner and cook, but to Ginny she was, in part, her mother, and they were close.

Libs sparkled—ebonized and energized—she was alive. She attended most of Ginny's family gatherings. She always prepared the food and washed dishes afterwards. She felt more comfortable in the kitchen even though she was as much a part of the family as anyone else. If you wanted to talk to her, you had to peel a potato or slice a tomato. It reminded me of the conversations I had with my mother beside the stove. It is in the kitchen where many great thoughts are prepared and served, and Libs delivered an abundance.

I remember her often standing in front of a sink washing piles of dirty dishes. Growing up, I never washed dishes; my mother did most of them, but I have come to enjoy washing dishes now partly because my wife's love language is service, and a cleaned dish is as good as a hug or a kiss. But I wash dishes for another reason. I like starting with a stack of soiled plates that I dip and scrub in dishwater, then rinse and put in a rack to dry. I start with something dirty and within seconds can restore it to its best condition. Then I can dry it, put it in a cabinet, and close the doors. After all is finished, I stand back to view a perfectly white enamel setting, whiter than snow. I am god of the sink, and I have made everything new again.

I have soiled relationships in my life. I have said and done things that have greased otherwise pretty plates and glasses. I have at times tried to put them in soapy water for cleaning, but sometimes it just doesn't work. I can't dry them, put them away, and close the cabinet door. They remain in my memory, still soiled and dirty. I do not have the power to fix everything that I have dirtied. I am not the god of my circumstances or my mistakes, so I wash dishes instead. I am in control of the outcome—the god of the sink. Libs washed a lot of dishes, which could simply have been just another job to be done to pay the bills, or perhaps she also wanted to be goddess of the sink where she controlled the outcome. Her first husband got her pregnant and abandoned her to raise their deaf son alone. Her son, ultimately, could not speak either. She adored her second husband, but he died very early in their marriage leaving her a widow for life. Maybe washing dishes gave her, as it does for me, an opportunity to make a tiny part of her world right.

Libs was soft spoken, but carried the big stick of prayer. She never said she prayed; she always said, "I was just talking to God this morning." She often spoke beneath her voice, and if you didn't listen carefully, her words were missed. Occasionally she exercised her will in dramatic ways. Once, during a family Christmas get-to-gether, the conversation centered around the usual topic of the most recent trip to Uganda, concerning something in the mission field. Ginny's father, Alfred, had not wanted to return home for Christmas because he was driven to accomplish the task set before him there, and he was bemoaning having to return, when Libs piped in, "I talked to God about your returning to be with your family this Christmas."

To this, Alfred responded light-heartedly, "Do you really think God listens to a prayer like that?" It was not really a question. The room grew still.

Libs quietly chuckled to herself and spoke with an agitated authority. "Ya here, ain't ya?"

The room exploded in laughter. Alfred grinned generously.

We entered her church that July morning for the foot-washing, full of anticipation. Most of the ladies dressed in white, every stitch white. They wore gorgeous hats with ribbons upon ribbons. Most of them adequately filled the garments to overflowing. In contrast, the men's clothing hung limply on their well-worn bodies. It was apparent who did most of the cooking and eating.

The pastor settled the congregation with a raised hand. He took his handkerchief from his shirt pocket and began dabbing his brow, which he continued doing intermittently throughout the sermon. It was hot and only a flurry of hand-held fans kept any movement of air. He taught about having a song in the night. The temperature continued to rise, and the sweat poured profusely down our faces, dripping off of our noses. The sermon moved like a beautiful piece of music, building until it reached its crescendo, delivering a message to the core. It was clear; we all needed a song during the midnight hours of our lives. They understood this; I only a novice to hardship. The "Amens" ringing out that day came from another time and place, from a people who were aware of their past.

Lib's congregation sang like nothing I had ever heard before. I remember the first time I heard Ray Charles sing *America the Beautiful*. He transformed it into an entirely different message. When he sang, the piano became inaudible and the words unnecessary. He sang the essence from his soul, and it echoed a song of hope in the night. This congregation did the same as they sang without accompaniment, but it sounded like a full orchestra. When they finished, there was no need for any further preaching.

The pastor returned to the pulpit and stood motionless, and a strange eeriness settled in, a quiet anticipation, like waiting on a hot summer's day for the bass to bite. Without any direction from anyone, the men brought white enamel basins half-filled with water and placed them beside each row, where they were passed down to all participants. This took a lot of time, which seemed longer in the heat of July. Finally everyone had access to one of the small foot baths. The men returned to their positions around the room.

Another silence.

The pastor raised his hands to heaven, and with a simple command, "Commence," the world turned topsy-turvy. Simultaneously, feet belonging to the young and old found themselves in the water in the white enamel basins. What happened next was otherworldly. The women began crying, then laughing, then wholesale, glorious emotion, raw and real. They jumped up on the benches and fell backward over pews where the men, dressed in black, caught and dragged them to safety in the corridor. Some women ran around the room, caught up in the spirit, others just quaked where they stood. This went on for several minutes.

We were only observers, but we felt pulled in to the power of it all. I forgot that my son, Graham, was sitting beside me. Sensing his presence, I glanced down to my side and caught his expression. His eyes were bigger than saucers, mesmerized and fixed. No fear, just amazement. I bent in his direction to make sure he was okay. When I got face to face with him, he looked at me and calmly whispered, "Daddy, that water must be awfully cold!"

That was all it took. I don't remember anything else. My eyes were fixed on my innocent boy who had sized up the situation as well as any six year old could. He gathered in all of the external stimuli, processed the activity surrounding him, and delivered the obvious conclusion: Cold water is a joy forever. It was Occam's razor in the hands of a child, and it was my first observance that my older son was a pragmatist.

We had the most delightful afternoon together with this new family. They accepted us immediately, and we talked and ate in the outdoors until dusk. In our white churches, we conclude church when someone says "Amen," and we all go out to eat in different locations. In black churches there isn't a conclusion, but rather a movement to a different location together for the remainder of the day and, for that matter, the week. They do church and life together, continuously.

Libs continued to live in public housing with her son. We visited her as often as we could. Her house was packed with furniture to the point that to travel from one room to another was to follow a narrow path between them. The walls in most rooms were decorated with unframed pictures of Jesus. The kitchen was small, made smaller because all of the counter space was occupied by boxes of food since the pantries were filled to overflowing with small, leftover packages of everything. The apartment smelled like there was a perpetual gas leak. We had it checked out, but nothing was ever discovered. Libs baked homemade rolls, but her gas stove always left that distinct flavor. They tasted like propane-infused bread. She always had some ready for us when we visited.

"Oh, Libs, I was hoping you'd have some of those rolls that taste like you made them," I always said.

Then I'd take a deep breath, put one in my mouth, and eat it as quickly as possible, without breathing, to show some measure of compassion to my olfactory.

"Have another," she urged proudly.

"Not for me, Libs. You know what the good book says. Man does not live by bread alone." No man could live by that bread alone. I was thankful I didn't smoke; one stray spark and the rolls and I would have exploded.

Libs taught Ginny that the temporal and the spiritual were synonymous. To iron and to pray were the same. She taught her how to fry chicken, how to correctly iron and fold handkerchiefs, but more than anything, she taught Ginny persistence, to keep on when the melody of the song in the night grew faint. She also shared her practical wisdom with Ginny as a child: "Now, Gin-Gin, it ain't so important if you are crazy in love with the man you marry, but he's got to be crazy in love with you. You can learn to love a man like that." Having had two husbands, an infatuation who abandoned her and a steadfast who adored her, she understood the difference.

She taught us all what it meant to speak the truth in love. She always gave a straight answer, and on those rare occasions when we truly wanted someone to tell it like it was, we asked Libs. Her inspiration was Frederick Douglass whose sentiments, "Agitate, agitate…" resonated with her. She was brutally honest. On one occasion when we visited her, I entered the front door and noticed newspapers strewn across the floor.

"Libs, do you want me to pick up these papers?" Her agitated eyes cut sharply toward me.

"Those papers are exactly where I want them, and you can keep your cotton-pickin' hands off of 'em."

"Yes, ma'am." This was the way I ended many of my short conversations with Libs. It meant that I had made a mistake, and I would never make that mistake again. You always knew where you stood with Libs, especially when you were on your knees begging for forgiveness.

But occasionally she played a bit of hide-and-seek with us, especially when it came to eating out at Captain D's, her favorite fine dining.

"Where do you want to eat today?" we asked, already aware of the answer. She never let on quickly, to keep us on our toes and provide an air of mystery.

"Just start driving and I'll let you know when it hits me."

Sure enough, just as we rounded the corner with Captain D's in view she said, "Well, let's try this place," and she chuckled. John nodded and smiled. He couldn't hear anything, but he had seen this scene played out endless times. We walked in, and she proceeded to the same table each time. She scrutinized the menu with deliberation and care. Finally, she carefully closed the menu, moving it to the corner of the table to signify the decision was made. The waiter came, and we all anticipated the same decision.

"I'll have the fish platter."

When it came, she eyed it pleasingly. Never in a hurry, she picked up the heavily battered fried fish with her long, bony fingers, gripping it like a chicken leg, and took small crunching bites, each one a delicacy. The napkin stayed prim and proper in her lap as she licked her fingers, one at a time. This went on long after the rest of us were finished. Finally, when every morsel disappeared, she gently reached for her unused napkin and gave it a one-time swipe across her mouth. Emily Post would have been impressed.

In her latter days, Libs continued to attend all of the family gatherings, not as a cook or a cleaner, but as a matriarch. Everyone crowded around her. She still had very little to say unless agitated about something that had happened at church or in the community. She occasionally surprised us with her rolls. Their aroma entered the house long before she did. She claimed they were from a secret recipe, but I knew they were two parts gas and one part flour. She continued to care for John, and they seemed more like brother and sister at the end. Little by little she shrank, not so much in spirit, but in body.

When she went to the hospital with serious complications, we visited her and brought fish when we could. It wasn't the same without the Captain, but fish on the docks was still pleasing to her. A large white bulletin board used by the nurses for instructions hung beside her hospital bed. On it we wrote: This is LIBS (Love In Brown Skin). The nurses raised their eyebrows at the inscription. She could be feisty, to say the least, and she had the capacity to voice her opinion forcefully on any topic, especially when she had a large audience. But when caught alone, her tired eyes reflected a calm refinement brought about by years of commitment to her son and her Lord. When she peered into our eyes, her agitation was converted to that love in brown skin, gushing out, flooding us with acceptance and genuine goodwill.

It was a terrible blow to Ginny when she passed away. Much like my relationship with my grandfather, Ginny's loss was saturating. The funeral was anticlimactic, as are most whose lives are honest and true. There was nothing inspiring about the curtain falling. Anyway, what can be said about someone who truly appreciated a good Captain D's fish platter, someone who made folding handkerchiefs a form of worship.

Her worldly possessions were measured by the pound. We cleaned out her tiny government-housing apartment and hauled off seventy-six large trash bags full of everything she had hoarded in fifty years. She had bags wadded up inside other bags. Anything that had passed through her hands, stuck. We found money placed here and there, in crevices, just in case, as I heard her say often. Ginny took care of much of their business, but she found twelve life insurance policies that Libs had paid on. Each was valued at less than what she had paid in.

Libs was John's interpreter to the world, and when she died he lost the ability to communicate. He tried, but she had been his only teacher. She alone knew his language. He had lived a lifetime in silence watching the world, a perpetual spectator. His value was not measured in his accomplishments; he had none, visibly, but his presence was undeniable. He occupied a very important place in his mother's heart, and he occupied a substantial corner of our memory. To exist in another's memory is to own a part of that person, and in that, John is always ours.

He lived many more years, but he grew fearful of everyone. We learned that there were those who took advantage of him, stealing from him as he walked to the nearby grocery. Finally he shut himself up inside his tiny home and depended only on the members of his church to bring him what he needed. When we came to visit, he refused to open the door. We peered through the window, trying to get his attention, but he ignored us, often hiding behind a chair.

Eventually, he was moved to a nursing home. When we first visited him there, it was obvious he was frightened. Ginny brought a bulletin board to his room and hung it beside his bed. She had gathered photos of his family and pinned them there; Libs was centermost. The familiarity provided some peace for him. Every time we visited, he pointed to it in appreciation and pride.

When he died, we were the only white people at his funeral. Ginny spoke. She had done so much to help him in his final days when he was alone. She loved John because she loved her Libs. His death marked the end of Lib's genetic line, except that we named our first child Hannah Elizabeth in her honor. In that way she lives on, and her namesake, with her own capacity for agitation, reminds us of this great lady and her quiet life that speaks so loudly to us today.

Several years later the tiny red brick government houses were torn down. The first time I saw the empty lots, my heart stopped. I was thankful they were going to be replaced by much nicer buildings, but the lot where Libs and John had lived had become, in my mind, an historic destination. It was where I met Frederick Douglass, in the unassuming fireball of a woman.

We have a picture, part photograph and part painting, of Libs as a child standing beside her mother in their Sunday best. It hangs beside my great grandmother. When I look at the eyes of each lady, I notice differences. My great grandmother's eyes are deep and penetrating. Her gaze is beyond the surface, like she is coming out of the frame. She wants to be part of this world. In contrast, Lib's mother stands, balancing her child on a chair as if in retreat in front of a curtain leading to a garden. She has no interest in coming forth. She enjoys the world in which she resides. It appears that when the photo was finished, she turned and walked away into the backdrop of the garden in which they are standing, turning her back on the present world. But the child's eyes are distinct, ready for the challenge. Those were the eyes we loved and admired so much.

She and John are both buried in Toussaint L'Overture Cemetery, named for the Haitian hero who led one of the few successful slave revolts in modern history. The cemetery was established a few years after the Civil War. When the trustees eventually died, the cemetery fell into neglect for decades. Finally, it was restored, but many tombs remained nameless. I am sure many were heroes like its namesake, but two particular ones stand head and shoulders above the rest: Elizabeth Crump (Love in Brown Skin) and her son, John.

CHAPTER TWENTY

We purchased Ginny's sister's art studio and brought it to the farm. We had no idea what we would use it for, so it sat abandoned and lonely for several years. Then Ginny decided to exercise her gift for hospitality by converting it to a bed and breakfast. We did everything required by law, and the Cedar Thicket Bed & Breakfast was born. Her talent in turning a worn-out building into a place of refuge was just short of awe-inspiring. In a short time, she decorated the interior with the necessities of making it cozy, comfortable, and quaint. She advertised it as a place where there was nothing to do but relax and enjoy the outdoors, which included gardens, woods, and a creek. And so it was. She built it, and they came.

Operating a bed and breakfast has its tranquil moments when congenial laughter flows unobtrusively across the front porch. Guest and host alike enjoy the warmth of the sunshine, and conversation reflects a simpler day when people took the time to listen to one another. We entertained guests from more than forty states in only a few years. Each visit introduced us to new people with interesting stories. Everyone loved the simplicity of the cottage and the surroundings. However, Southern charm has its limits, and occasions arise when split-second decisions made by the master of the house are necessary in maintaining balance in this world of reality.

We booked the cottage for an elderly couple and their two grandchildren. They had sought out a quiet place with animals in which to create some special memories—a Hallmark experience. They arrived late one afternoon, exited the car, and looked around in complete satisfaction. The children immediately ran off to view the sheep and the cows in a nearby pasture. We showed them around, telling them some of the history of the family. Ginny's sensitive hospitality was always comforting. She led them to the cottage where she had made every amenity perfect, every detail carefully thought out, every lamp dimmed just so. It was beautiful just walking through the front door. They loved every aspect. We left them to themselves, and we returned to our home, satisfied.

The entire weekend proved to be the complete respite the grandparents had dreamed. On Sunday morning, after enjoying another one of Ginny's wonderful breakfasts, the couple with their two adorable grandchildren meandered around the farm for one last look. Then, having packed away their suitcases, they stood around the car to say a last goodbye to Ginny and to thank her for the gift of that weekend.

I was inside our home witnessing this quaint scene. My mind drifted off, knowing we had provided the desired memory and it brought a small but significant smile. However, as I dreamily gazed in their direction, out of the corner of my eye I caught a faint vision of movement. Slowly turning my head, I saw a slinking coyote sauntering across the field just behind the Hallmark family. My familiarity with this vermin was recent. Something was killing my rabbits at night, and on one occasion I got a glimpse of the killer. He was before me now.

All rational thought left me. A Jekyll–Hyde complex took over, and my only purpose was to rid us, once and for all, this menace. I hastily reached for my twenty-gauge shotgun, which had belonged to my father. It was special as a reminder of the man who never used it. I, too, seldom used it, but when your father gives you something like a gun, it becomes a national treasure. The firing pin was actually the end of a pitchfork jammed in tightly, but it never misfired. It was a single barrel, so I quickly put one shell in. I was often asked why anyone would want a gun that fired only one shell, to which I replied, "One shell in the chamber is worth two in the hand." It didn't make any sense, but it was effective and they walked away confused and left me alone.

Sometimes a mission clouds one's perspective of the immediate world around him. Such was the case as I dashed past our guests with the anticipation of killing the beast. Only a few yards from the children and their grandparents, I planted my feet firmly in the sod, looked carefully down the barrel, and slowly squeezed the trigger. The sound of the explosion, along with the screaming howls of a now-mangled coyote, was sweet to my ears. As the smoke cleared, the culprit dragged itself into the trees behind the cemetery, shrieking all the way. The aroma of gunpowder and the triumphant feeling of success penetrated every pore of my body.

At that moment I had the exhilarating feeling of being the protector of our abode, a man standing bravely in the gap for the protection of his family, the king of the castle, the big-game hunter. I heard shouts of acclamation and cheers of .... It suddenly dawned on me that these sounds didn't exactly resemble a victorious mood. Something distinctively sorrowful wailed behind me.

Turning around, I viewed a frantic couple desperately trying to console their hysterical grandchildren. Apparently they had not received the same measure of satisfaction that I had. My eyes then cut toward Ginny for an explanation of this odd behavior. I may have been the king of my castle, but the queen was not happy. She had her eyes fixed on the gun with a peculiar grin usually associated with a madman on the brink of doing something desperate. She closed one eye and squinted like she was looking down its barrel. It unnerved me.

Suddenly she snapped back to the present and immediately made her way to the family. She was desperately trying to explain as she pointed in my direction, but they were already in the car quickly backing out of the driveway. I smiled and waved.

"Come back and see us anytime."

I was so happy to be a part of providing unforgettable memories for our guests. I could tell the children were heartbroken to leave, as hysteria was in full measure in the back seat. I wanted to stay there and bask in the glory, but the car kicked up quite a lot of dust as they left. I coughed and retreated toward Ginny.

She stood staring down the driveway. I knew she was disappointed to see them leave. Every time we had visitors, Ginny ended up getting to know them as dear friends. She made such an impression on our guests that we often received Christmas cards from these people who to me were only acquaintances. I ambled up beside her to offer my consolation. Tears ran down her cheeks. I put my arm around her shoulders, but instead of gently cushioning her head on my shoulder as she normally did, her torso was stiff as a board. This couple had affected her greatly.

"Can I do anything to help, Sweetie?"

She mumbled something indistinguishable and walked quickly toward the cottage to start the cleaning process. I began to think that running a bed and breakfast might actually be too much of a strain on her emotions. She was so sad about the couple leaving and the nostalgic weekend we all enjoyed. I repeated my insistence to help, but she walked away at an even quicker pace.

"I need to be alone for a while" she said numbly.

These are the times that try a man's ability to comfort the savage beast that lies deep within the heart of a woman. I needed to give her words of hope and a promise that the sun would rise again.

"Don't worry, Sweetie, there is another family coming in a few days, and I'll be here to help." At this she stumbled slightly and disappeared into the cottage.

What would she do without me? I mused.

That night in our bed, she explained in detail how that might be arranged.

CHAPTER TWENTY-ONE

After three years of farming the land of my ancestors, I decided to leave it. My best-laid plans from childhood had changed. The best part of farming is being with family, but the main farm was two miles away from our home. I left each morning at four-thirty. I came home for meals, but I spent most of the day, ending at about six p.m., away from Ginny and our daughter, Hannah. It seemed inconceivable to walk away from the only occupation I ever intended, but it was equally inconceivable to do it without them. The last year I worked the farm, my brother joined me and we worked together. The plan was for him to buy me out at the end of the year. During that time, I explored every possibility for my future employment, but it was futile, and I became depressed. Perhaps I had made the wrong decision.

One evening after supper, I went out, sat on the back steps, and looked up at the beautiful night sky with its canopy of stars. I said a simple prayer. "Lord, give me something I can do with my family." It wasn't a prayer about changing the world, or becoming the Great Stone Face, or leaving some imprint on humanity. I just wanted to be in the presence of those I loved the most.

I finished the year out, transferred everything to my brother, and then I was on my own. I tried my hand as a nutritional consultant in the dairy business, but it eventually died out. Then one morning about six I was standing by the window when a school bus drove by. It was a foggy morning, and I could barely make out its passing by. I only noticed the driver and one small head on the otherwise empty bus. My heart sank. The thought of this little child riding a bus so early going to school away from home, not returning until evening, was heart wrenching. That would be Hannah in a few short years.

That was the beginning.

At that time I was teaching a youth group at church every week, and I went to a room full of middle school students who had been sitting in exactly the same formation all week at school, listening to someone speak at them. And I was the final act at the end of their school week. It seemed cruel to make them go through this on Sunday. I hated it as much as they did. I thought how great it might be to get them outside under a tree or on the banks of a creek where so much of my education occurred. I finished my quasi teaching that year and swore I'd never do it again. But something kept tugging at me.

I cannot discern fiction from non-fiction. Reality is gray. The universe teems with endless beauty and possibilities, and since I am a part of it, everything is wide open, anything is possible. As Mary Oliver succinctly prophesied for me, "The world I live in is much wider than that. And besides, what's wrong with Maybe."

The day I asked Ginny what she thought about starting a school, she looked at me with a strange expression, similar to eyeing down a shotgun barrel. I remember it because when, in the future I came up with other unusual ideas, it was that expression I looked for. It says, *You are crazy, nobody in his right mind would consider such a lame idea … but just maybe.*" She was homeschooling Hannah at the time, and she understood more than I did the commitment required in doing this thing we refer to as education.

"Do you have any experience teaching?" she probed.

"None, except that bunch of boys in New York, you remember the boy whose neck I stretched?"

"What actual qualifications do you have?' she continued the examination.

"None, except that I attended The Webb School where all the Rhodes Scholars went."

"Is that it?" Her voice sounded frenzied and frantic.

I had anticipated her question and had prepared a speech. It reminded me of the days in high school when I entered oration contests, so I proceeded to orate to her about my time there:

"When I arrived in Bell Buckle in 1971, my only objective was to retake the eighth grade so I could gain weight and stature enough to return to Riverdale High School in Murfreesboro to play football. I came from a home where athletics and farm work trumped books. After one year at Webb School, though, I forgot about football. I was mesmerized by the learning atmosphere. There was something different and wonderful about the place, and I wanted to get to the bottom of it all. It was primarily through the influence of five teachers I received my qualifications as a teacher.

Mrs. Crowe was a robust woman. She taught eighth grade English in a poorly lit room next to the old auditorium in The Big Room. She introduced me to words through her unusual approach. Each week we received a new list of vocabulary words. We did the traditional workbook stuff, but then she told us we could gain extra points if we saw these words printed or if we heard someone speak them during the week. We thought she was crazy. All we had to do was speak these words to ourselves or write notes to each other using the words throughout the day until we had enough points to earn that coveted A in her classroom. We considered her a fool beyond measure. *Did she not realize she was dealing with highly intelligent Webb School boys?* We played her game, and we all ended each quarter with a 100 average. We took full advantage of this poor, ignorant teacher.

I do not how much later it was that it dawned on this highly intelligent Webb School boy that I had been duped. She had played the fool for my benefit. She tricked us. I learned more vocabulary that year than any other year of my life. She was glad to give us what we thought was important in order to give us something so valuable that we could not see it. I grew to love words in a way I did not expect. They excited me, and she was the catalyst. She taught me that a great teacher gives away a part of herself for the benefit of the students. To play the fool, to become obsolete, is the goal, and she did it with an unassuming genius.

As a freshman I descended the stairway and entered Mr. Alexander's biology classroom. It was his first year as a teacher. He had just graduated from Harvard, and he wanted to give something back to a school he regarded as having given him his education. The unusual part was that his degree was not in biology. Quite the contrary, it had something to do with writing, we were told. On the first day of class, he peered over his spectacles with the kindness and calmness of an old professor and told us he did not know that much about biology, but he was excited to learn with us. I was struck by his honesty. Throughout the year, he dug in deeply with us as we explored the world of microbes. On many occasions, we asked questions that he said he also had. Then he proceeded to tell us of the research he had done the previous night. He anticipated our questions, and in doing so he made inquiry a viable pastime. By example, he led us into the world of knowledge. We disregarded the grades we were receiving. They became insignificant, but surprisingly, we all did well anyway. We were learning. More importantly, we were learning how to learn.

This is what Mr. Charles Alexander taught me about teaching. It is not important to appear superior. After all, he was a Harvard graduate; he had every reason to snobbishly look down upon this runny-nosed group of boys. But he showed us that humility is the most important aspect of an educated person. He taught us that to be educated is to know enough to realize how little one knows. He came down from the podium and came into our world, showing us how powerful it is to be a part of a student's education. He offered me a place at his table of knowledge, and we dined together.

My sophomore year found me in the geometry class of Mr. John Lewis Morgan. He had taught just about every subject related to the sciences at Webb over a number of decades. Now nearing retirement, he taught only geometry which he called "jomtry." On the first day of class, he went around the room asking our names. With most of the students, he had taught their fathers and in some cases, their grandfathers. These were prominent names around the southeast. When he got to me, I proudly stood up and declared, "I am Gilbert Gordon, sir." I could see his wheels turning, but nothing was coming. He was struggling to boot up information that did not exist. Finally he said, "That's a fine name. Live up to it."

Mr. Morgan and Euclid, the father of geometry, were contemporaries. They had spent a lot of time together, and Mr. Morgan shared their relationship with us. His class had little to do with finding numerical answers to math problems. Anyone can find the area of a circle with the right formula. No, Mr. Morgan had a broader view of the queen of math. Proving that a triangle had 180 degrees was the essence. It did not matter that it had 180 degrees; it had to be proven. And thus we entered the world of the proof. Each day we were called to the chalkboard to submit our method of proving the particular problem of the day. Although I loved the thinking behind it all, my proofs were generally too long, and they involved a lot of circular reasoning. What took my peers five steps in a proof, I needed a dozen.

Mr. Morgan called me to the board one morning to write up a relatively simple proof. I took thirty minutes, and I covered the entire board with white chalk. When I finished, I stood back and proudly viewed the definition of superfluous. Mr. Morgan looked it over for quite some time. I could tell he was trying to find the right words. Then he walked up and put his hand on my shoulder and said his immortal words, "Well, there's more ways to kill a dog than chokin' him on hot butter." I wasn't exactly sure what it meant, but his genuine smile made me believe I had succeeded. He always looked for the good in his students, and he always found a way to encourage us. Mr. Morgan taught me to look for the silver lining in each student.

The antithesis of Mr. Morgan awaited me in my junior year when I entered Mr. Russell Norvell's junior English class. I was petrified because of the stories that had leaked out about him. Mr. Norvell was a realist, and he was brutally honest when it came to assessing an essay. He knew how to tear you down and build you back up within the minute. He was not concerned about feelings; he wanted us to learn to write. Books could be written about Mr. Norvell and his methods, but one particular idea was his PARA approach to writing. He paired two people together; one was to come alongside the other as a mentor. I was paired with my younger sister, Teresa. After a couple of weeks, he called me into his office and said my sister was imitating my writing. I thought it was a compliment. I smiled and said thank you. It was a big mistake. He exploded. Then he explained that good teaching was not about making other people into clones. He taught me that great teachers guide in general directions and leave the rest to the traveler. Mr. Norvell was not one to control. He expected a lot, but it was always in the context of making us better communicators. "Only connect," he would say.

By the time I reached my senior year, I was convinced that I knew about everything there was to know and did not need any further instruction. So when I sauntered into Mrs. Truitt's calculus class, I sat in the back row and leaned the chair back against the wall with an accompanying attitude. I made immature sounds. My favorite was the sound of a beating heart. It was actually pretty good. Mrs. Truitt knew where it came from, but she was wise and ignored teenagers in general. She was wonderful, even to an arrogant eighteen year old. She always dressed rather professionally, and she began the class at the chalkboard where she got so involved that soon her entire wardrobe was covered in white. She was never aware of her appearance when she taught. Although she was young, her hair had early streaks of gray, besides the chalk, which actually highlighted her dark olive complexion. I loved the pitch of her voice; it reminded me of a sine curve with its peaks and troughs. It sounded like a young boy whose voice was changing. I also loved her wild eyes and bushy eyebrows.

She made calculus come alive for me. Soon I was not sitting in the back row, and my noises had ceased. I will never forget the day she told us we could determine the volume of a doughnut using calculus. I had actually considered it in Mr. Morgan's geometry class, but I concluded it was impossible because when a cylinder is straightened there are gaps. So when she showed me, I was ecstatic.

Once, she called me into her office because of a poor grade on a test. I was six foot two, and she ... wasn't. I looked down on her, but I was looking up at a teacher I had come to love. She could be tough, and she told me she was disappointed in my work. She never said she was disappointed in me, but my work. Now I would do anything to keep from disappointing her, and the remainder of the year I worked in that direction.

In the early 1970s, these five teachers and others at Webb regarded education as an undefinable, mysterious part of life. They made ACTs and SATs pointless, an inconvenience. They were getting at something bigger. They were largely unsung, but for this farm boy whose mother drove the bus to pay for tuition, they sparked in me a love for learning and a desire to pass that love on to others. It was at Webb School that I obtained my teaching degree. I had witnessed it firsthand from the best. Teachers make a school, and these remarkable men and women made Webb School a great place of learning and helped me become the person I am. Perhaps even I could teach."

It was a great speech, and I looked to see if Ginny was impressed. She wasn't.

"Teaching is one thing, but what makes you think you can start a school?"

She had me there. Then she added, "You have lived your entire life in this area, and many people know you." I thought she was building a very substantial case against anyone sending children to a school I started. Then she surprised me and said, "You are well respected ... it just might work." The very words my father had used years before. Six months later, we founded Cedar Hall, a one-room school. Thirty years later, the dream remains.

There have been many wonderful aspects to having a school on our farm, but none more than the time I have had with my family, especially my wife. This was the answer to my prayer. Ginny and I spend all day together. Most days we are never more than a hundred feet apart, and at the end of the day our experiences are identical; we wear many similar hats. Rarely does anything happen that we don't already know. So when we frequented our favorite restaurant that night, we discovered we had spent far too much time together.

As we dined that evening we noticed people talking, laughing, and gesturing about undoubtedly something exciting that happened during the day, and they seemed to be exuberant about sharing it with their dinner partner. We looked at each other, trying desperately to muster up some semblance of enthusiasm, but we already knew everything that had transpired during the day. It was like trying to surprise myself with something new. But we tried.

"Well, Sweetie, how was your day?" I asked

She stared at me blankly, and then her eyes twinkled and a slight grin, and then a somber, serious look I could not read. She looked down at the table and then her sad eyes looked deeply into mine. "Well, Gilbert, something rather extraordinary happened today." I sat up inquisitively.

"This morning," she continued, "while I was in the library all alone, the principal of the school came in, trapped me in the corner, grabbed me around the waist, and began kissing me." She hesitated, looked down, and continued, "I enjoyed every minute of it. I'm sorry."

Silence, and then, leaning forward in my chair, "Did you have any idea he felt this way for you?"

"I strongly suspected it, but today he told me he has loved me since he first set eyes on me, that he can't live without me, that I am the most beautiful and intriguing woman he has ever known." I sat back in my seat, then responded.

"I must admit he has good taste. Was that all?"

"Yes, but after school I had a similar experience with the janitor, and it seems I am always attracted to the same type of man."

A prolonged silence, and then I asked, "Well, where do we go from here?"

"Just take me home, Gilbert, I need some rest. Tomorrow I have a date with the groundskeeper."

Marital affairs are satisfying when they are with the same person you said "I do" to.

But not all dreams come true. When I drove down Rock Springs Road on my bike preparing for the Olympics as a fourteen year old, every dream was within my grasp, but life has a way of letting the air out of the tires. Although the school we founded was originally for grammar school students, we also operated a high school for twenty years. This came at the requests of a few fervent eighth graders. It was based on the Great Books schools, primarily St. Johns College in Annapolis, Maryland. I had high hopes it would be an example to the world. It's just the way I think. Everything has to be a blockbuster event.

We had trouble keeping students, due in part to my lack of foresight. Finally, after 19 years, we had to close that part of the school. It devastated me. My mother was still living, and somehow I had to tell her that I had given up and quit. I could hear her from my youth saying, "You can't quit; we don't do that sort of thing."

When I told her, she smiled and said what I should have expected.

"You did your best, and there are times when you have to move on. I am so proud of you and Ginny." And she was; she told us often.

At the last graduation, my emotions were mixed. I was so proud of our son, Carter, and what he had accomplished. This was his night, along with the other five graduates. I wanted to do something unique, so I told them at the beginning of the year I had a very special surprise for their graduation night. I hoped this would counter the disappointment of the closing.

I wrote to Harper Lee, author of *To Kill A Mockingbird*. I asked her to come to our final graduation. I told her about the school, its philosophy, and its closing. I added that I made great biscuits we could enjoy with molasses after the festivities. I thought this would attract any Southerner. I asked her not to return an answer; I just wanted to hold on to the hope she might appear. I needed this to help me get through the year. Anticipation is life-giving. The strange part of it all was that I never doubted her coming. It didn't matter that she had not given interviews in fifty years. Dreams are no respecter of facts. I was back on my bike headed for the gold medal, and the tires were aired tightly.

The night of the graduation, which occurred in our front yard, I saved two chairs in the front row with a sign that read, "Reserved for Special Speaker." I was asked about them, but I just smiled in anticipation. I couldn't wait to see the look on their faces when Harper Lee walked up and sat in her reserved place. It wasn't until five minutes before the ceremony that I began to wonder. I wasn't really worried, but it would be awkward if she were late. I kept looking at each car that passed, hoping it would turn in.

But it didn't. She never made it.

The graduation was spectacular, filled with tears and laughter, and everything we could have hoped for. Everyone was honored. The party afterward was a culmination of everything good that year. As the last car drove out that night, I went to the front porch and sat down, still puzzled. I just hoped she wasn't lost somewhere between Rock Springs Road and Alabama. I still couldn't bring myself to believe the obvious. I knew she meant to be there but something came up. She wasn't in the best of health.

For months, even years afterwards I expected to get a letter from her telling me why she was unable to attend. Then she died. That should have ended it, but I still thought I would receive a lost letter that she had meant to mail. I am a fool's fool, but I don't mind. As Abraham Lincoln said, "Whatever you are, be a good one." I'm still waiting.

Once, I submitted a poem to the Prairie Home Companion Valentine Sonnet contest. I wrote one I thought would win. That night we listened to the top ten. I wasn't that impressed with some of them, so I was confident I was going to capture the prize. With each reading, approaching number one I grew more hopeful and excited. It was inevitable. Finally the winning sonnet was read, but it wasn't mine. It didn't make sense. Ginny went upstairs and used the telephone to call back downstairs. When I answered it, she impersonated Garrison Keillor's voice with amazing clarity. He (she) said he really liked my poem the most and congratulated me. I actually believed it. She felt badly for me when she told me what should have been obvious to any rational human being. I felt badly for her, having married such an idiot.

And now I have written a book. The first edition only included part one. I intended to print 100 copies and give them to family and friends, but Ginny insisted on 250. So we started distributing them first to family, then to our community and other friends. I was embarrassed giving them something that required their giving up time to read. I just hoped they would find something redeeming in it, but my expectations were low. Then I started getting responses, overwhelmingly positive. These were not, "Thanks for the book, I liked it" responses, but a sincere love for the book. I was stunned.

Now my dream–nature exploded, as usual. It wasn't enough to have written something meaningful for my friends. Now *Ramblings* was destined to become a bestseller, whatever that means. As my expectations grew, so did my anxieties that everyone would read and praise this highly acclaimed work. It consumed me to the point that my value as a person was tied to every comment I received, and when friends did not respond, I grew depressed and wondered why they did not like the book and, by extension, me. I had made dreams my god. Totally blind, I couldn't see the forest or the trees. It also affected my relationship with Ginny. Marriage is more about presence than proximity, so even when we walked hand in hand around the farm, my mind was often engaged in rearranging a paragraph or finding a better word. I abandoned her as we strolled together. I replaced the art of living with the art of writing, all in the name of being a Someone.

Isn't the world supposed to stop and acknowledge me? Isn't someone going to say, "Aren't you the Gordon whose great grandfather ... Didn't you go to Webb where all the ... "*Didn't you write ...* "

Thankfully, it never happened. Miss Emily Dickinson was there again when I needed her.

I've come full circle now. The second part of this book has been a true joy to complete. I am writing for myself again, and not for recognition. Words are wonderful in themselves. I will publish this, complete with part two, and have it on my shelf as a reminder that any dream becomes reality simply by attempt. Results are never a measure of success. Rudyard Kipling was right, "If you can meet with Triumph and Disaster and treat these two imposters just the same." I came full circle, but I returned a different person, and it was the journey itself that acted as the catalyst.

Dreams are still good. They denote a sense that the world is bigger than we know, that there is something strange and wonderful waiting behind door number three. Disappointments accompany dreams in some measure, but the only way to avoid them is to avoid expectations, and that is poor living. Dreamers fly higher than the pragmatic crop duster. The higher the altitude the less we make of the complexities of daily living. But sometimes dreamers do an Icarus and get too near the sun, and reality melts away the wax on our feathers, and when a dreamer falls, it is a long way down.

I never felt more fully alive as a child than the times I played with marbles in my grandfather's front parlor. Lying on my side, left arm cocked, supporting my head, one eye on my grandfather, the other fixed on the marbles, I would take one out of the cigar box, place it on the top of a slanted plank and release it. I watched it gain speed until, reaching the bottom, it came to a halt on the carpet. I did it for hours, mesmerized. When I took my first high school physics class, I learned the names of what happened to marbles rolling down a slanted plank. It was potential energy, then down an inclined plane, then kinetic energy. The knowledge didn't increase the excitement of rolling marbles, but it led me, as an adult, to put a few things together to know myself better, which is, I suppose, the point of education.

So, the potential energy of a marble in its youth at the top of the plane is at 100 percent. It is completely absorbed in looking at the future and what might happen. As it rolls down the incline and enters middle age, it loses potential energy (the future loses its grip as the exhilaration of the present takes over). Reaching the bottom, it has no more potential energy (the future loses its allure). But the fullness of the kinetic energy is complete (the present is sufficient). The net result of all of this is that I don't dream as much now. My potential has all but been converted to kinetic. Unfortunately, this has produced a vacuum in my daily living that frightens me. I miss the potential, the dream, but I am learning to fill that emptiness with present moments in simple ways, but even still ...

I haven't told anyone this, but sometimes at night when I can't sleep, I tiptoe downstairs into our den, turn on a lamp, and stand before our small library. I'm looking for something to read. So

I pass by many of my favorite poems and books. With indecision, my hand gently fingers one after another until it lands on a small book with a beautiful cover.

"Oh, I wonder what this is?"

And I pull *Ramblings* off the shelf and peruse the front and back nonchalantly. Then I lie on the couch and open up to the sections that make me laugh and cry. I reread certain passages, reminding me of the people I love and of the labor required to make the language pleasing to my ear. Everyone should write a book or create something that can be tiptoed to at night when no one else stirs, to hold in your hand something you created, regardless of its worth to anyone else.

And the thought comes: *I wonder if on a sleepless night someone else will tiptoe to a private library in a den and run searching fingers across favorite poems and books and finally land on* Ramblings. *Then gently take it to the couch, lie down, and read a favorite story or perhaps a paragraph that is meaningful, something that gives the night radiance. Perhaps a smile will move across a face, maybe a tear or two in the solitude.*

It's possible to imagine in the world in which I live.

"And besides, what's wrong with Maybe."

CHAPTER TWENTY-TWO

Today Ginny and I live in the Old Home Place and are the caretakers of the family cemetery. I remember when I was only a boy that our cemetery was nothing but a series of groundhog holes and fallen gravestones. No one had cared for it then. It was my father who took the initiative to contact the family, raise some money, and bring it back to its former status. He accepted the responsibility of taking his turn in providing for his ancestors. My father was truly a great man. But now it is our turn.

Efficiency at times finds its way even to the home of the dead. Although a feeling of reverence accompanied me while cutting the grass, I still had another life, and I needed to finish the job as quickly as possible, allowing ample time to live life among the living. One isolated gravestone sat very near the border fence. It made cutting difficult because I could not wedge the lawnmower between it, which increased the amount of weed eating. I decided it was time to move it, so I retrieved a wheelbarrow, and little by little loaded it. The tires were almost flat as I wheeled it up to the crest of the graveyard where I deposited it behind the old maple tree. It would go unnoticed there. Besides, I did not know this person, and no one had ever visited him. His name was Joe B. Bailiff, and he died at age twenty-one. That was all I knew.

The next month an old Lincoln Continental pulled into our driveway. The door creaked open, and an elderly man gingerly pushed himself out of the seat, taking a minute to straighten up, and then looked around to see if he was at the right place. He saw me coming out of the house, and he raised his hand to acknowledge his presence. I met him, and he asked only, "Is the Gordon cemetery around here somewhere?"

"Yes, it is," I said, pointing to the elevated knoll with the cedar trees.

"Would it be okay if I walked up there?"

"Of course, I'll go with you." I loved hearing stories from men like him. They were a treasure trove of life experiences. Their voices were like ancient texts slowly fading away. It took us some time to ascend the small incline, as he struggled with each step. He appeared deep in thought, so I kept a little distance as I walked slightly beside and behind.

We entered through the black iron gates, and he ambled methodically up and down the rows of tombstones, reading each one audibly. With each stone, his anxiety grew. He read until he became frantic. His gait, which had a limp to it, picked up momentum. Finally, he spied a flat piece of stone near the fence. He made his way there, and without looking at me asked, "What happened to the stone that sat here?"

"His name was Joe B. Bailiff," I said, "but I don't know who he was, and no one remains who remembers him. I moved his gravestone behind the maple tree over there to make my mowing easier."

He stood there for some time as he gathered himself. "This is my brother. Could you move the stone back?" He was not angry, just matter of fact.

I moved quickly. It took a wheelbarrow to move it the first time, but I hastily made my way to the maple tree, stooped down, and did a bear hug around the stone. I think I heard a few vertebrae pop, but there was more at stake than a backache. I placed it back where it should have been and apologized profusely.

He said nothing for a while, then he spoke, staring at the stone.

"We were very poor in those days. Every day was a chore just to survive. We didn't own anything. We were sharecroppers and lived in a tenant house. Didn't go to school much. Had four brothers, three sisters. We didn't have money for doctors. My brother died of appendicitis, I think, … not sure."

He stood, envisioning an old world. A thousand images paraded before him as he smiled, then grew solemn, and smiled again. I felt uncomfortable imposing on his time with his brother, so I slowly backed away. He immediately looked over his shoulder and said, "Please don't leave, it was your family who gave us this space. You should be here." So we stood for the longest time, silently enjoying each other's company, two people who had just met, but whose ancestors had tied us together in such a remarkable way that I felt I had known him forever. He had invited me to his family reunion. There were three of us.

Time stops in a cemetery; nothing ever really changes. It had been more than sixty years since he had seen his brother's gravestone, but it appeared he had just been away for a week or so. He finally nodded to his brother and said something under his breath. Then he turned to me, smiled, and said he needed to go. I apologized again, but he reaffirmed it was unnecessary and thanked me for the well-keeping of his brother's resting place. He ambled back to his car and left. I remained behind.

Left alone, I took a moment to take a different perspective of this sacred ground. I took a panoramic view. On the opposite end was a gravestone of a man who survived WWI. He fought on the front lines, enduring the freezing weather, the tear gas, the flame-throwers, and the hopeless fatigue of war. Triumphant, he wrote home to his mother that he was alive and would be home on the next ship. He had thwarted every attempt to destroy him. He had survived, but he did not realize he was no match for a virus. He contracted the Spanish Influenza and died, along with millions of others. His mother received him as a corpse.

Stuck between these two men were two children, each a victim of drowning. The first was a three year old from a distant relation, the other was my brother's only child, who drowned in Dry Fork at precisely the spot where my grandfather and I fished underneath the great willow tree. He was buried between where my brother will be and where his mother is now. There are other children who died in infancy, some at birth. The stones are small, but I'm sure the grief of the loss was just as large as others who lived a century, perhaps greater.

Dr. A.N. Gordon's tomb is inconspicuous. He was the last doctor in our community, delivering most of the children. He was also a counter of votes in local elections. Gordons were staunch Democrats to the point that the words "Republican" and "aristocrat" were synonymous, and the Democrats were out to save the common man. On one occasion after a particular election, Dr. Gordon was counting the ballots. After more than a hundred votes for the Democrat, a Republican vote came to his attention. A bit perturbed, he registered it and continued to count. Then another Republican vote came up. He immediately stood up and exclaimed, "Just throw them both out, the son-of-a-bitch voted twice."

Then there are the eccentrics, none so much as my Cousin Margaret. After her husband died suddenly of a heart attack, she lived alone for twenty years. She eventually moved to a nursing home, where Ginny and I had the privilege of seeing her often. Her smile was electric, and her optimistic view on life was healing. I could visit downcast and melancholic, and she, by her very nature, lifted me out of it. In her final months, she became totally blind, but even then, light emanated from her spirit, and she shone just as bright.

She was also a Democrat, primarily because her son was a successful member of the U.S. House of Representatives for many years, representing our country and, more importantly, our family well. Her love for her son vastly outweighed her overall disgust with politics, and she was his staunchest supporter. I asked her once who she thought our best president was. In ninety years, she had witnessed more than fifteen of them. I thought she would have a good perspective. She contemplated the question for a while. Her glorious smile went awry, and she said, "Well, it might have been Bill Clinton, if he had kept his pants on." I was drinking tea, and I spewed it over the room. The conversation ended as we all laughed together. Even in politics, Cousin Margaret generated glee.

The weather was horrific the day she passed away, and it didn't change for more than a week. So much rain fell that the gravediggers were barely able to dig a hole. On the actual day of her burial, there were only a few who weathered the storm, and the burial crew could only partly fill the hole. She was quickly lowered into the soupy mud, and they placed plywood over the top, temporarily, until the rain let up, which they hoped was the next day so they could cover her properly. It didn't let up, and it rained for another week.

When the sun finally emerged, I put on my high-water boots and sloshed up to the cemetery. As I neared the gate, I couldn't help but smile. Cousin Margaret, much like my mother, had an indomitable spirit with a sense of humor for any situation. The casket, which had been so carefully lowered the previous week, was now halfway out of the ground at a forty-five degree angle, like a sinking ship before it makes its last gasp and disappears beneath the waves. The adage was true—you can't keep a good woman down. My mother had the remarkable ability to get the last laugh, but even she could not extend this talent from the grave. Cousin Margaret had accomplished the impossible. She entertained us from another world. In the back of my mind I heard a faint melody, then it burst forth, "Up from the grave she arose!" I just stood there and took it all in.

In addition to the visible stones, a line of invisible graves exists down the corridor of the cemetery. It is only through the stories passed down that we know of them at all. These were people who were even poorer than Joe B. Bailiff. They died with no family, and were buried in unmarked graves with only cedar poles placed in a triangular form over them. In time, the poles rotted, and no traces of them remained. They were, in the words of George Eliot, "to the number who lived faithfully a hidden life and rest in unvisited tombs."

A casual glance, and I saw my direct descendants lined up in perfect chronological order. I can pace fifty feet and cover nearly two hundred years of my family's history, beginning with the man from North Carolina who freed his slaves, to those who endured the Civil War, down through my grandparents, my father and, of course, my mother.

My mother is cleaning the house.

She works there quietly as I play outside.

I come inside to get a cold glass of ice water from the refrigerator.

But there are times I come in, and I can't remember why I'm there.

So I pass through the room where she is cleaning,

Or the kitchen where she is cooking,

Or the office where she is paying the bills,

And I stand … and I can't remember why I'm there.

So I brush near her without words and return to my play—
a happy child.

My mother died and was buried in the family cemetery behind
my home.

She lies there quietly as I work around the farm.

I go there to cut the grass or pull the weeds or trim the
dead branches,

But often I walk through the black iron entrance gate,

And I can't remember why I'm there.

So I make my way up the gradual incline until I stop where she
is sleeping.

And I stand … and I can't remember why I'm there.

So I brush near her without words and return to my work—
a contented man.

My happy places are generally where I am accompanied
by my special people. A creek bank is only a creek bank without
my grandfather. A front porch swing is only a front porch swing
without Mrs. Eunice. A stove becomes a tabernacle in my mother's

presence, and this final resting place, filled with those I have loved and who have loved me, makes this another one of my happy places.

Cemeteries are living places. They tell the stories of real people who lived, and loved, and dreamed, and ultimately found a resting place worthy of the struggle. I have measured off the exact spot where I will be placed someday. I lie down there in my perfect rectangular area and try to imagine what the weather will be on that day. I prefer spring, when the daffodils are in full bloom, and the sheep graze the early spring clover. Then again, I could be content with autumn, when the leaves are changing and first frost makes for a crisp afternoon. The summer has its benefits as well, with its view of garden squash and beans and a mass of watermelon vines. But, you know, winter is probably most appropriate, with its dormancy, leafless maples among the beautiful cedars, knowing that spring is near, and resurrection is just around the corner. I hope it isn't raining; I have a phobia about sinking ships.

I took one last look: the farmers, doctors, writers, athletes, poets, lawyers, soldiers, rebels, and children. I made my way back to the house, the home of my ancestors, who lived here and cared for this place while they could, as best they could. They watched the innumerable caravan making its way to and fro at death's invitation, until it was their turn. Then the duty was passed to the next generation.

For now, it is my turn to care for this family. Who can say when I will be ushered into their presence? I'm in no hurry, but death is not so much a mystery anymore. It will be a dream come true to meet firsthand this Christ I put my trust in. I don't expect

He chews tobacco, especially on Sundays, but I'll bet that when He sees me, He will erupt through His smile and say, "Gibut, you wanna have some fun?" Then I will realize I was a Somebody all along, and I will be free, finally free, to enjoy life's next big adventure.

Then someone else will take over the duties of the cemetery. They will cut the grass, and pull the weeds, and pick up the dead branches. They will drive their lawnmower around and in between and look at the stones, and the dates, and the names. They will brush near, and when they come to mine, if it hasn't been moved behind the maple tree, they might wonder who I was, and they can find their copy of my book on a private shelf late one night and read this account of my life and the people who enriched it, and be reminded that there's magic in our ramblings, that some dreams do come true, and no one's life is inconsequential.

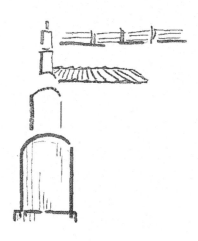

The Beginning

ABOUT
THE AUTHOR

Gilbert Harrison Gordon spent the first half of his sixty years on his family dairy farm. The last thirty years have seen him turn to teaching as his vocation. He and his wife, Ginny, founded Cedar Hall School on a part of the family farm in 1991 and were privileged to teach their own children while they taught others. Teaching still brings them both joy and purpose as they continue their 'ramblings' on Rock Springs Road.

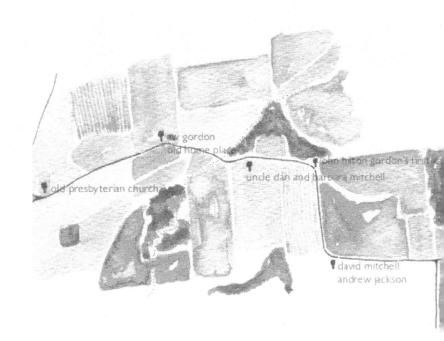

mallard house

charles and catherine gordon
gilbert's birthplace
miss eunice